MANYA'S
Story

MANYA'S *Story*

Faith and Survival in Revolutionary Russia

Bettyanne Gray

Foreword by Nora Levin

RUNESTONE PRESS MINNEAPOLIS

RUNESTONE PRESS · ᚱᚿᛏᚼᛏᛉᛏ

rune (rō͞on) *n* **1 a** : one of the earliest written alphabets used in northern Europe, dating back to A.D. 200; **b** : an alphabet character believed to have magic powers; **c** : a charm; **d** : an Old Norse or Finnish poem. **2** : a poem or incantation of mysterious significance, often carved in stone.

Copyright © 1995 by Runestone Press
a division of Lerner Publications Company
241 First Avenue North
Minneapolis, MN 55401

Library of Congress Cataloging-in-Publication Data

Gray, Bettyanne.
    Manya's Story : faith and survival in revolutionary Russia / by
Bettyanne Gray ; foreword by Nora Levin.
      p. cm.
    Previously published : Minneapolis : Lerner Publications, © 1978.
    ISBN 0–8225–3156–9
    1. Abramson, Manya Polevoi—Juvenile literature. 2. Jews—
Ukraine—Biography—Juvenile literature. 3. Ukraine—Biography—
Juvenile literature. 4. Jews—Persecutions—Ukraine—Juvenile
literature. 5. Ukraine—History—Revolution, 1917–1921—Juvenile
literature. [1. Abramson, Manya Polevoi. 2. Jews—Ukraine—
Biography. 3. Ukraine—History—Revolution, 1917–1921.]
I. Title.
DS135.U43A254 1995
947'.71004924—dc20   94–32393

Manufactured in the United States of America

1 2 3 4 5 6 – I/JR – 00 99 98 97 96 95

For My Circle of Life—
My Mishpucha

My beloved husband, Don
Our worthy children
Ellis and Donna Gray
Heidi and Angelo Devita
Debi and Dan Waskow

Our cherished grandchildren
Charles Jacob
Aaron Michael
Jacob Matthew
Elizabeth Manya Rachel
Mason Alexander

And to my rebbitizen Hilda Riback,
my devoted teacher, my loyal friend,
an insightful mentor who has inspired,
guided, and enriched my entire adult life

"A gracious woman obtaineth honour."
                                                —Proverbs 11:16

CONTENTS

FOREWORD

The broad historical setting of *Manya's Story* is one of the most turbulent periods of the 20th century. The events of the years from 1917 to 1921 snuffed out the lives of millions of people in Europe and the hopes and dreams of millions of others. Human suffering was immense and widespread. Jewish suffering was especially severe because of the ravages of war in the Pale of Settlement (the region in western Russia to which Russian Jews were confined) and because of sudden shifts of power that made Jews the pawns and victims in a maze of conflicting forces.

Ukraine was the crucible of suffering for the Jews of Russia. This area within the Pale of Settlement had witnessed intense anti-Jewish feelings and murderous pogroms in the past; during the chaotic period following the Russian Revolution in 1917, anti-Jewish violence again swept through Ukraine. Three forces—the Bolshevik Red Army, the anti-Bolshevik White Army, and the Ukrainian Nationalists—contended for control of the region. Caught between these opposing forces, the Jews of Ukraine were subjected to vicious and bloody pogroms, primarily at the hands of Ukrainian and White Army soldiers. Between 1919 and 1921, when Bolshevik control was finally established, more than 2,000 pogroms took place in 700 Jewish communities. The number of Jews killed, maimed, raped, or orphaned was around 200,000, over 10 percent of Ukraine's Jewish population.

As the Soviet forces progressively consolidated their power in the early months of 1921, Ukraine was reoccupied and a certain measure of security for Jews was restored. Many of the members of Manya Abramson's family who survived the pogroms remained in the Soviet Union to undergo the rigors of life in a Communist society, the restrictions of Soviet anti-Semitism, and the horrors of World War II. But Manya, her husband, Israel, and their infant son, Valodya, were able to escape and begin new lives in the United States. The story of their escape has been handed down to Bettyanne Gray, Manya's American-born daughter and the author of this book, who has had the pain of knowing about her family's experiences while being spared the experiences herself.

I have felt a special attachment to Manya Abramson's story ever since I first heard it told by Bettyanne Gray in my class at Gratz College in Philadelphia. My students and I were spellbound by Bettyanne's account of her family's experiences. I am sure that every reader will be gripped as I was by its portrayal of the miracle of survival in a death-drenched world and of human love enduring in the midst of great adversity.

—Dr. Nora Levin (April 1978)
Noted scholar and author of *The Holocaust* and *The Jews in the Soviet Union since 1917: Paradox of Survival*

A Chronology of Events Relating to
MANYA'S STORY

1914

June 28

Austria-Hungary declares war on Serbia following the assassination of the Austrian archduke Franz Ferdinand by a Serbian radical. Entangling military alliances draw other European nations into the conflict, leading to the outbreak of World War I.

August 1-4

Germany declares war on Russia and its ally France. Great Britain joins the conflict against Germany.

1915

Russia's early military successes turn to failure. German troops invade and occupy most of the Pale of Settlement, the vast area in western Russia (Ukraine) to which Russian Jews had been confined since 1794.

1916

The war continues to go badly for Russia. Thousands of Russian soldiers desert because of food and arms shortages. Strikes and riots occur in the cities. Czar Nicholas II, influenced by the mystic Grigori Rasputin, refuses to make needed reforms in the government.

December

Rasputin is murdered by a group of nobles. Russian political groups of all persuasions express their opposition to the czarist government.

1917

March 1-11

Bread rationing is introduced in the Russian capital of Petrograd (now St. Petersburg). Food riots and strikes follow, and the soldiers sent to stop the disturbances begin to join the rioters.

March 12

The czar attempts to dissolve the Duma (parliament). A Soviet of Workers' and Soldiers' Deputies, made up of representatives of workers, soldiers, and socialist groups, is established in Petrograd. The Soviet assumes leadership of the anti-czarist forces and forms an uneasy alliance with the Duma.

March 15

Czar Nicholas is forced to give up the throne. The Duma sets up a provisional government, headed by Prince George Lvov. The Pale of Settlement is abolished.

April 16

The exiled Bolshevik leader Vladimir Ilyich Ulyanov (better known as Lenin) returns to Russia, determined to overthrow the provisional government and to bring about Russia's withdrawal from the war.

July

An uprising of workers and soldiers protesting the war is seen as an attempt to overthrow the government in Petrograd. Lenin is held responsible and is accused of working with the Germans. The Bolshevik leader goes into hiding in Finland, and Alexandr Kerensky, a socialist, becomes premier of the provisional government.

September

General Lavr Kornilov, the army commander in chief, attempts to seize power. Kerensky frees imprisoned Bolsheviks and allows them to arm the Petrograd workers against Kornilov. The general's coup fails, and the Bolsheviks win a majority in the Petrograd Soviet.

October

Lenin returns to Russia.

November 7

The Bolsheviks sieze control of the Russian government. Three years of civil war and allied occupation lie ahead of Lenin and his followers before they will be able to extend their power over the whole of Russia.

November 20

In Ukraine, the Rada (parliament) refuses to turn over power to the Bolsheviks. Instead, the Rada proclaims the establishment of the Ukrainian National Republic and begins to organize a government that promises some degree of freedom to Ukrainian Jews. Jewish members of the Rada vote approval but have misgivings. They fear a takeover by anti-Semitic forces, who have been responsible for anti-Jewish riots during the preceding months.

1918

January

The Rada declares the independence of the Ukrainian National Republic. Bolshevik troops invade Ukraine. Unable to obtain protection from Ukrainian troops and viewing the Bolsheviks as a foreign army of occupation, Jews form self-defense units.

February

The Ukrainian government signs a separate peace treaty with Germany. German troops take over Ukraine and drive the Bolsheviks out. Anti-Jewish pogroms, or massacres, continue.

March

Russia and Germany sign the Treaty of Brest-Litovsk. Russia withdraws from the war and concedes much territory, including Ukraine, to the Germans.

April

The Germans dissolve the Rada and set up a Ukrainian government headed by Pavlo Skoropadsky.

November

Germany is defeated by the Allies. The territory of Ukraine is returned to Russia, and the Skoropadsky regime collapses. A five-man Directorate is established under the leadership of Simon Petlura. Armed conflict breaks out between the Bolsheviks and the Ukrainian forces. Some of Petlura's soldiers carry out frightful massacres of Jews.

1919-1920

Ukraine is caught up in a struggle for power among three forces—the Bolshevik Red Army, the White Army (Russian opponents of Bolshevism trying to prevent the consolidation of Bolshevik power), and the Ukrainian army. As a part of their struggle with the Bolsheviks, the Whites and the Ukrainians unleash waves of pogroms against the Jewish population of Ukraine.

1921

The Red Army defeats the White Army and the Ukrainian forces. As the Bolsheviks gain control of Ukraine, pogroms diminish.

1922

The Ukraine becomes the Ukrainian Soviet Socialist Republic, an integral part of the U.S.S.R.

Manya's Story

PROLOGUE

I am a first-generation American whose parents, Manya and Israel Abramson, were survivors of two vicious pogroms in Russian Ukraine during the years following the Russian Revolution. After narrowly escaping death and losing everything they had worked to build, my parents were forced to leave their homeland in 1921. They came to the United States, seeking not solely to live, but to be free to live as Jews. During World War II, the family they left behind paid the extreme penalty for desiring nothing more than this right to live as Jews. Invading Nazis murdered more than 200 members of our family clan in Talnoye (called Talne by residents) in Russian Ukraine, leaving only a handful of survivors.

As a youngster I listened, petrified with horror, to the grim tales of slaughter in revolutionary Russia. Each time I heard them, I hoped the vivid details would be less gruesome. But time could not alter the terrible facts.

When World War II began, I was a child in South Philadelphia. I reacted with terror to the whispered rumors of the Holocaust. My parents spoke of it in tones of veiled mystery. Apparently, unbelievable as it was, crimes even more monstrous than those of the pogroms were being committed against the Jews of Europe.

I recall the ashen faces of my parents as they spoke about it. They were consumed with anguish and worry over those whom they had left behind in Ukraine. They had had no contact with Talne since the outbreak of World War II, but they surmised that what was happening elsewhere in Europe could be happening in Talne. And indeed, the worst did happen.

The agony of the Holocaust never left my mother's mind. She spoke of it tearfully and was tormented by nightmares. In a vivid dream, her relatives directed her to honor the memory of the Shmuel Ber-Brucha Polevoi clan members who had perished and to establish a memorial for the tragic circumstances of their death.

My mother was so affected by this dream that she set aside a special day each year to recite Kaddish for her relatives. On August 24, 1974, my mother, Manya Polevoi Abramson (later known as Miriam Frank), met with her entire family at Congregation Brothers of Israel in Trenton, New Jersey, to remember the almost total destruction of the Polevoi clan. A plaque in their memory was unveiled and a memorial service was led by Rabbi Howard Hersch. Before my mother passed away, her last request was that her descendants continue to recite this special Kaddish.

It is significant that my mother's last request was not for personal remembrance but for the continued fulfillment of the pledge she had made to the memory of her martyred family. And yet, I could not overlook a request that she had made of me years before. She had urged me to record the story of her own experiences in Russia before the Communist takeover of Ukraine.

Ukraine was my mother's birthplace and her home for the first 24 years of her life. During my lifetime of intimate companionship with her, she told me vivid stories, both of the warmth and joy of traditional *shtetl* (Jewish village) life and of the agonies suffered by the Jews during the Russian civil war and the Ukrainian nationalist fight. It is these stories that I sought to preserve and record. And so, in memory of my dearly beloved mother—my best friend and revered mentor, a devoted daughter, and a woman of valor—I fulfilled my promise with the writing of this book.

In the years since the book's publication in 1978, I have rediscovered many relatives now living in the United States. Members of the Polevoi clan read the book and contacted me when they recognized family names and photographs. The reconnection of this extended family of Russian-American Jews has shown how important the remembrance of our shared history is to all of us.

I hope this new edition will help my grandchildren and all generations of Polevois to cherish this legacy and to value our free and democratic land of opportunity. And I hope readers of all backgrounds will gain empathy for oppressed people who struggle even today to live in freedom and safety.

With this new edition, I hope my expanding family, the mishpucha, will understand not only Manya's life but the lives and values of all Russian *shtetl* Jews. For the importance of these recollections, beyond their personal impact, is not that my parents' experiences were unique, but rather that they are representative of the histories of countless Jews throughout Russia in the early part of this century.

The impudent gather themselves

together against me;

Not for my transgression, nor for my sin,

O Lord.

Without my fault, they run and

prepare themselves;

Awake Thou to help me, and

behold.

Psalms 59: 3-4

*I*t was the fall of 1917. Even simple pleasures were difficult to devise with the country engulfed in a world war. With the German invasion of Russia, the whole flow of Manya Polevoi's life was altered. So far, the fighting was a long way from her home in Talne, a tiny town in the lush wheat fields of Ukraine. Yet everyone there felt the threat of war. A cloud of waiting hung over them. There was nothing to do but pray that Talne would be spared, and that normal life would soon return to the *shtetl*.

For Manya, the days were endless. With most of the young townsmen off fighting, there was little relief from the monotony of her life. One morning she sat in her room, idly brushing her mass of black curls. She stretched each tendril and let it recoil, gently coaxing the ringlets into first one position, then another. Critically, she examined her pretty face and figure in the three-way mirror. Although she was frequently teased for this preoccupation, she enjoyed studying herself. Now, smiling with genuine self-satisfaction, she approved the vision facing her. She had repeated this scene countless times. What young man, she wondered, would be a match for such a splendid young woman?

At 21, Manya was lovely and inviting, but in remote Talne

there was not one man she would consider giving the honor of loving her. And now, with the war halting private travel, she couldn't even entertain the idea of visiting her out-of-town relatives in the hope of attracting some handsome stranger. So another morning passed, and she spent it fantasizing and lamenting the utter waste of it all.

Today was Friday, and the Jews of Talne were busy attending to last-minute details before the Sabbath. The square bustled. The Sabbath traditionally began at sunset. Now, with winter approaching, the sun set earlier each day, and so the Sabbath began earlier than in the summer. This meant heightened activity on Friday mornings. Although most of the women were home cooking and tidying, the square was full of people by 10 o'clock. Grandmothers, daughters, and the few young men who had managed not to be drafted into the army crowded the shops and stalls. Usually Manya and her best friend, Esther Gorchman, made it a point to be there, laughing and shopping in the throng. But even the promise of this small amusement was not enough to entice Manya this Friday. Pointless meanderings in the square had no appeal for her, and she had no errands to accomplish. All last-minute marketing would be attended to by her grandmother, Bubba Brucha, who had assumed this chore when she had moved in with her son Yosel and his family.

So on this particular Friday, while Manya was at home, Esther was at the square alone. She did not mind being by herself, knowing that within minutes she would be approached by one of her many acquaintances and asked to join them. Esther was regarded as very pretty, although a bit too delicate. No doubt her widowed mother found it hard to feed and clothe herself and her daughter on her small earnings as a tailor's helper. Yet Esther managed to dress nicely by capitalizing on her mother's skill with the sewing machine.

While Esther waited for her friends in the marketplace, Manya contentedly puttered about her bedroom. It wasn't often that she could have it to herself. She shared the room with her older sister, Ruchel, who was with her boyfriend Pavlusha today, attending one of his revolutionary political meetings. Her grandmother, who also shared the room, was about to leave for the market. Soon the room would be Manya's alone for the day, and she didn't intend to leave it for an instant. Manya pulled on her pantaloons, then her petticoat, and finally her embroidered undershirt. Her grandmother helped, as usual, by pulling at the laces of Manya's waist cincher. Once dressed, Manya silently delighted in the fact that she did not need to stuff the front of her shirt for fullness as her sister Ruchel did. But it was small compensation. Ruchel, two years older and hot-tempered, managed to remind Manya almost daily that though she was not as tall or shapely as Manya, she had a prettier face. Among the Polevois, it was acknowledged that Ruchel was the family beauty.

Manya consoled herself with the knowledge that she was gentler and of a sweeter disposition than Ruchel, who was given to rages and outbursts of temper. Yet, while that helped a little, it could not completely ease the ache of knowing that Ruchel dominated the affection of the house. For it seemed that when she entered a room, everyone was startled by her beauty and enchanted by her elfin quality. Manya, too, felt involuntary delight in just gazing at her sister. But still the resentment could not be stifled.

The clang of the door chimes interrupted Manya's thoughts. She did not hurry to answer. Instead she went down the stairs slowly, running her hand along the polished wooden banister as she went and admiring the depth of the grain and the lushness of the honey tone. Like everything in her family's home, the wood was of the best quality. Manya's father,

Yosel, a well-to-do furrier, had designed their home. It was an impressive double house fronted by four stores. The two on the right were leased to Mr. Greenberg, a jeweler, and to Beryl Radelsalski, who operated a custom leather goods store. The two stores on the left were used by the Polevois themselves. One store housed Yosel's fur business, which had been in the family for several generations. The other was a drugstore that was run by Manya's brother Boorah.

In designing and building his home and shops, Yosel Polevoi had created an ideal master plan for a most remarkable piece of real estate. Nothing in all of Talne matched the style, grace, and practical function of the Polevoi establishment. Manya felt pleased as she thought about the Polevois' position in the community. Majestically she glided toward the door across the fine, polished wood floor. But when she heard Esther's impatient voice shout, "Manya, Manya, have I got news!" she hurried unceremoniously to greet her.

Esther, her cheeks aglow, was bouncing so excitedly that her tangled braids flew about her head. Manya giggled with anticipation and waited for Esther to calm down.

At last, Esther contained herself long enough to blurt, "There's someone new in town! I met him at the square this morning!" She paused to catch her breath, then continued. "He's a pharmacist from Odessa, and he's going to take over the management of Boris Petrofsky's drugstore now that Boris has been drafted. His name is Israel Abramson, and he doesn't have to fight in the war. To avoid being drafted in Czar Nicholas's army, he pulled out some of his teeth and cut the tendons of his toes, so that he limps. But he's gorgeous! He's about six feet tall and has black curly hair. His eyes are blue as the heavens in June, and he's very smooth and literate. He quotes Talmud and Mishnah—but he's not ultraorthodox."

With a nudge, she added, "In fact, he's very liberal in many ways." And she allowed a vague giggle to erupt. Then her mood shifted and she said quite seriously, "But he's mine, Manya. I saw him first. I'm seeing him tonight, and I beg you not to play games."

Manya tensed. She sensed Esther's anxiety and wished to reassure her friend. They both realized that the pale daughter of a poor widow was no match for Manya and that the only way for Esther to win this unsuspecting young man was to ask Manya to keep her distance. Out of compassion and loyalty, Manya pledged her solemn word not to interfere. She also promised to help in any discreet way she could. So when Esther asked if she and Israel could use the side veranda of Manya's home that night, Manya meekly consented. It was risky for Esther, but she could not bear to invite Israel to her own shabby home.

Inwardly, Manya was angry with herself. If she had not spent so much time in her room that morning admiring herself, she would have met this young stranger. It would have been Manya Polevoi who had a rendezvous on the veranda. Her father had built it especially for "his girls," and now Esther would use it before her! She balked at the irony of it. But, bound by her affection for Esther, she promised her full cooperation.

When they parted, Manya felt a strong need to be diverted, so she went straight to Boorah's drugstore. There she was met by Meyer Zaslovsky, a young clerk, who led her into the rear laboratory where Boorah was working. As Manya glanced around, sniffing the familiar scents of herbs and perfumes, she thought of how often she had wandered in here when she felt restless. She thought, too, of the constant visits she had made to her father's shop downstairs. She loved the smells of Papa's shop even more than those of the drugstore, for she had lived with them longer. They were among her earliest recollections. She smiled to herself as she recalled the bustling action in the shop upon her father's return from his ventures. His travels took him to many countries in search of the best lambskins and fox and lynx pelts, which he used to trim fashionable garments.

In fact, Yosel was off on one of his trips at that moment. He had been gone more than three months, and the whole family felt anxious. He had been due home a week earlier and had not yet come.

How Manya longed for his return! With all the fighting going on, this was a terrible time for a business trip. She almost wished that he were not so influential. For it was his influence that had enabled him to bribe certain officials into giving him transit papers, which were virtually forbidden to Jews. Some of these officials had been on the family payroll since the days when Manya's grandfather, Shmuel Ber, ran the fur business.

Manya remembered how much she had always delighted in Yosel's return. How she loved her father's tales of his journeys, and how he loved telling stories to her! Manya was an enthusiastic listener, and her face always mirrored her enjoyment as she listened to her father.

Enveloped in her pleasant memories, Manya kissed Boorah absently. He was working at a polished marble counter in the laboratory. She idly picked up a recipe and read the list of ingredients aloud, reaching for them as she named them. Carefully, she began to prepare an herbal potion. As she was blending the compound, Boorah swept her aside.

"You ninny! You stick your fingers into everything! You tell Papa how the men should sew the fur, you steal into the kitchen and show the maid how to keep order, and if I'm not careful, you will be the next manager of this store! Now, get your hands out of this mixture. Think of how mortified I'd

be if people said that you could do my job as well as I. Scat!"
He scowled mockingly.

With that, Manya threw her arms around him, and they
both laughed. She enjoyed this "lecture," for she liked to be
reminded that she was an excellent manager around the
house. Then, too, she enjoyed her brother's teasing. "I love
you, Boorah," she said simply. "And I love you, sister," he replied with equal sincerity. Brother and sister embraced for a
moment. Then Boorah returned to his work, and Manya left
as abruptly as she had come.

Manya's visit with Boorah had been only a diversion. Now,
she could not keep the matter of Esther and this prince of a
suitor from surfacing in her thoughts. The thing to do, she
decided, was to take a long nap and to dismiss the subject
from her mind entirely. The fellow was probably a beast anyway, with his self-imposed handicaps. No doubt it was
Esther's boredom and longing for romance that gave him
such appeal. With that thought for consolation, Manya returned to her room.

Dominant in Manya's personality was her sense of fair-
ness, and Esther had nothing to fear from her. Still, Manya's
curiosity caused her to imagine all sorts of potential intrigues.
With discipline, she secluded herself in her room, determined to sleep and forget. She hoped that she would awak-
en purified of all shameful notions. She slept fitfully.

After some time, sounds of laughter and squeals of joy
reached her drowsy brain. She sat upright in her bed and listened for a moment. Her father was home! Manya pushed
aside the mountainous goose-down comforter and bounded
down the stairs. Overflowing with excitement, she flew into
her father's arms. Whatever foreboding she had had earlier
now evaporated in the pleasure of seeing her father after
more than three months. This Sabbath would bring the whole

family together at last. The Polevois all shared a love for family unity. Tonight their home would be a holy sanctuary, and their table would become an altar graced by the ceremonial Sabbath lights. There could be no more fitting way to celebrate their beloved Papa's return. With thanksgiving in their hearts, they would sing the *Kiddush* and recite the *Hamotzee.*

Drying tears of gratitude, Manya's mother, Leah, said, almost reverently, "Everyone, dress with speed. I'll light the candles within the hour and there will be time enough for talk and questions." She and Yosel embraced happily and slipped away together.

Channa and Mikhail, the two youngest children, could not wait to begin rummaging through the silks, jewelry, and exciting parcels that their father had brought home. The gifts were not as plentiful as they had been before the war, but still there was a treasure or two for each child.

Bubba Brucha was overjoyed at the safe return of her son. Contentedly, she busied herself in the bedroom she shared with her two eldest granddaughters, while the girls fussed with their new Sabbath garments. As usual, Ruchel had managed to get the better bolt of cloth for herself and had ordered the dressmaker, under threat of dismissal, to make her dress more elaborate than her father had prearranged. The finished dress looked more expensive than Manya's in every way, and Manya fumed. Papa would hear about this! Tonight she would point out the differences in their clothes, and surely her father would recognize Ruchel's obvious guile. But she would hold her tongue until after dinner. She would not risk dampening the mood of exhilaration sweeping over them all.

Eastern Europe at the end of World War I. The shaded section on the map indicates the location of the Pale of Settlement, the area to which Russian Jews were confined from 1794 to 1917.

Above: *A rooftop view of Talne*

Below: *The Polevoi family conducted its business in the two stores on the left side of this building. Yosel's fur business occupied the space on the lower level, and Boorah's drugstore was on the upper level. The family's home was located behind the stores.*

A portrait of the Polevoi family taken in 1912: (standing from left to right) *Mikhail, Boorah, Manya, Israel (Yosel's brother), Ruchel, and Channa;* (seated from left to right) *Leah, Bubba Brucha, and Yosel.*

Brucha Polevoi—"Bubba Brucha"

Manya

Ruchel

*A*t dinner, the shadowy candlelight quieted Manya's spirit. After the blessings, the first course was served by the Polevois' maid, Masha. Leah was still busy in the kitchen and, according to their own family traditions, no one lifted a fork until she was seated. Only when Leah joined them did Yosel handle his silver. This was the signal for the others to begin.

As they ate, Yosel talked about his trip. He had seen and heard much about the war and about the Russian political situation in general while he had been away.

In March, Czar Nicholas had been ousted and replaced by the Socialist provisional government. The new Socialist leaders, Alexandr Kerensky and Prince Lvov, had been conducting Russia's war with the Germans. The Bolsheviks, led by Lenin and Trotsky, had been busy organizing against the provisional government.

The current government's management of the war was going badly. The Russians were losing, and the army was thoroughly demoralized. Young boys had been ruthlessly drafted and, without any training or experience, had been shipped immediately to the front lines to die. It was as if Russia were trying to hold its boundaries by lining them with dead bodies. There were countless deserters, and officers were killing their own boys, who were retreating from certain death. It was very bad—bad beyond description. The Germans would occupy all of the area near Talne within weeks.

But Yosel had heard that the Germans were being very civilized and efficient in their takeover of other towns. They were only interested in claiming Russian resources, not in killing, raping, or burning villages. Yosel assured the family that their lives were safe. And after listening attentively to him, they began to wonder if German rule might be kinder than the heavy hand of the czar had been.

As Masha cleared the table and set up the samovar for tea, there was a soft knock at the side door. It was Esther, looking ethereal in her special dress, with an unsure air that was at once pathetic and appealing. Manya explained to everyone that she had offered Esther the side veranda and asked that no one disturb her. Everyone agreed cheerfully and wished Esther luck. So while the family was having tea, Esther and her young man sat outside on the veranda, laughing in hushed tones and enjoying the crisp autumn weather.

After a time, the curtained french doors opened unexpectedly. Esther stood nervously next to a young man who was surely the handsomest to have ever set foot in Talne. He extended a warm, hearty handshake to Yosel and, flashing an irresistible grin, announced, "To accept the hospitality of such a fine veranda from an anonymous host is just too much. I'm having a marvelous time, and I insisted that I be allowed to tell you so personally. Excuse me if I am intruding."

Yosel was obviously impressed by the fellow's poise and candor. Manya was intimidated by his brashness. The village boys she knew were not so forward, so confident, or so over-whelming. She sat quietly with lowered eyes, lifting her lash-es only to acknowledge the introduction as her name was mentioned.

Leah fell into the role of hostess and invited Israel and Esther to tea. Israel promptly accepted for Esther and him-self, and the rest of the evening was pleasant for everyone. But even though Manya did not encourage Israel, Esther saw that he was attracted to her friend. She knew she had unwit-tingly handed him to Manya, but she was the only one who knew. And though Manya was not to blame, Esther hated her hopelessly.

Two days later, Israel stopped by Boorah's drugstore. He wanted to discuss with Boorah his new post as manager of Boris Petrofsky's drugstore. He was greeted by Meyer Zaslovsky, who told him that Boorah was having his meal with his family.

"By now even Channa and Mikhail should be finished chatting, so be patient," Meyer told him. "Lunch should be over shortly. Wait if you can." Israel decided to wait, and passed the time in conversation with Meyer. Making small talk, he asked, "Have you a girl?"

"In my heart, yes—in reality, no," Meyer answered. "I have admired Manya Polevoi since the year before my *bar mitz-vah,* but she wouldn't look at me then and she doesn't know I exist now. And who can blame her? There is no compari-son between her station and mine. I have nothing to offer a girl like her. In these times stranger matches are made, but in this case it won't happen, I can assure you."

"Too bad," Israel replied offhandedly. He wondered to him-self what kind of girl Manya was to cause Meyer such misery.

When Boorah came back from lunch, he and Israel began to talk shop. They discussed continuing a business arrangement set up by Boris Petrofsky when he had managed the shop Israel had just taken over. Under this arrangement, Boorah and Israel would help each other. If either was out of a product, rather than lose a customer to any of the three other drugstores in the village, they would lend stock to one another. After shaking hands on what promised to be a mutually beneficial agreement, Israel added, "Incidentally, I really enjoyed your family the other night. I am one of 10 children, and we are all very close. My father died when I was just a year old, and my eldest brother Samuel raised us all. I miss my family—but much less so when I'm in such warm company."

"You're welcome any time, Israel. I mean that," Boorah said sincerely.

Israel's eyes lit up. "Good!" he said. "Tell Manya I'll come by soon."

"Ah!" smiled Boorah knowingly.

With that, Israel sauntered off, his limp barely noticeable.

At the Polevoi house, it took the family several days to adapt to having Papa at home. Routine had not yet set in; there was still a bubble of excitement that no one hastened to burst. Tea after dinner was especially holiday-like, for it was then that they had many visitors. The Polevois had relatives by the score in this village—200 at least. In groups of 5 and 10, they came to see their rich relation, to welcome him back, and to glean some information about the war. They talked, ate, and enjoyed the bonds of their heritage. It was a scene they repeated often that winter.

Though there was peace and contentment in Talne, in the big cities everything was in upheaval. The Bolsheviks had at last succeeded in overthrowing the provisional government and establishing a Communist government. At the same time, the war with Germany had continued throughout the winter. It seemed that sooner or later such events would have to touch the people of Talne.

Then one night in March, when the Polevoi house was filled with cousins and their families gathered around the samovar, the festive mood was broken by a wild pounding at the door. It was Israel Abramson. He gestured excitedly for silence and attention.

"The Germans are in Talne!" he cried dramatically. "The Bolsheviks negotiated with the Germans last week, and on the third of March, Trotsky signed the Treaty of Brest-Litovsk. This whole territory was conceded, and the Germans are taking over the entire area. Ukrainian crops and livestock are being confiscated. German officers have commandeered this village for their administration headquarters!" He turned excitedly to Yosel.

"In the absence of Rabbi Twersky," he asked, "can you, as *gabai* and *shtuut balabos,* tell us how to deal with this? Shall we run, fight, or give up?"

There was no thought of resisting, as no one had weapons or ammunition. Yosel replied calmly. "Israel, the Germans have a highly organized, superbly trained force. Their officers are career soldiers with a strong code of honor. As I have said before, they are not killing and raping behind the lines. They want Ukrainian material and food, and they'll take them as the spoils of war, but our persons are safe. Our streets will not become a battlefield." Then he said kindly, "Calm yourself. I see that you're upset. Stay here with us, and we'll see what will happen. I can assure you, this will not be a pogrom."

Yosel poured several glasses of schnapps for the men as they prepared to leave for the square to hear news. He put on his black coat and hat to go with them. But before anyone could leave the parlor, three uniformed Germans appeared in the doorway. They walked slowly across the wood floor, noticing the finery—the silver, the china, and the ornately engraved samovar. The senior officer said in German, "This home has been appropriated by the German army and has been assigned to the three of us by the Kaiser's instructions. We wish you no harm. Our days will be spent attending to military business. At night we require meals, beds, and hot water for bathing. Other than that, we ask nothing. You may continue with your daily routine. We seek friendship and we offer it. We regret this imposition, but it is unavoidable. Actually, it is one of the lesser tragedies of this war."

That announcement began a whole new way of life for the Polevois. The soldiers moved in that night, and suddenly Yosel Polevoi was no longer master of his domain. But even in bad luck there are degrees. These captors were well-bred men, and within days after the soldiers moved in, it was clear that life could go on and could even be tolerable. Once the fear passed, a tentative friendship emerged. Zigmund, the senior officer, was a born aristocrat. Although he was not obliged to, he saw to it that he paid his way by buying food for the entire household. Before the war, Zigmund had been a noted writer and orator. He had a cultivated wit, and his German was understandable to the family because of its similarity to Yiddish. The children especially loved his stories. In a short time, everyone seemed to forget how he had come among them, and they began to enjoy his presence.

Zigmund also enjoyed the family and loved to tease Israel and Manya. By this time they were a romantic twosome, and Esther had given up the precarious claim she held on Israel. Now when Israel came to call, he preferred the privacy of the side veranda to the companionship around the samovar. He and Manya didn't notice the cold weather at all, and throughout the winter they had enjoyed the remote veranda in spite of frost and snow. On a typical evening, Israel would come to call on Manya. Stamping and shaking off the snow, he would greet everyone and ask for her.

One night Zigmund said, "Israel, you'll have time to drink a bottle of vodka before she comes down, at least if she's still in front of her mirror!"

Everyone roared. Zigmund put his hands on his hips and sashayed from side to side as if posing in front of a mirror. Israel was convulsed with laughter, for Zigmund did indeed capture Manya's stance.

But after they had all had a good laugh, Israel remarked soberly, "Careful how you make fun of her. I hope to marry that one."

Many nights were spent in such warm friendship. But one night on the feast of Purim, their pleasant evening was abruptly interrupted. It was after the *seudah*, and Masha was passing around a tray of *hamantashen*, the sweet pastry dessert that was traditional for that holiday. Suddenly, a German soldier in a corporal's uniform barged into the house.

"Show me the way to Captain Zigmund and be quick about it," he commanded. Zigmund quickly came out of the kitchen, where he had been telling Leah one of his humorous stories. Now, he dropped his relaxed manner and assumed the role of the German officer he was. After a brief, curt exchange, he and the two other soldiers in residence grabbed their guns and went off into the night.

The Polevois felt apprehensive for the safety of their "boarders." These soldiers had shown them every courtesy and had continually offered apologies for intruding on them. But now danger was imminent. Even though the Russian government had made a treaty with Germany, many Ukrainian farmers' lands had been confiscated. They had been robbed, taxed, and belittled by the Germans and still fought back whenever possible. Thus ambushes were frequent. Tonight, blood would spill. The vanquished would have revenge.

The next morning only two soldiers returned—Zigmund and one aide. The other officer had lost his life in a street skirmish. Though the house was heavy with mourning, none of the traditional mourning customs were invoked. The soldier had not been a Brother of Israel and not even a townsman. But he had been a kind occupier who had become a comrade of sorts. He had been at their table, had learned their blessings and recited them, and had broken bread with them and joined in their laughter. Now death returned him to the gentile world, and the local priest was called in to perform the funeral rites. The body was taken away.

It was a genuine loss to the Polevois. While it was not the kind of tragedy that brought an outcry of anguish, it did engulf them with a quiet desperation at the circumstance that had robbed a good man of his life. Their only comfort was in the certainty that this was God's will.

The family had lost one friend. The other two officers remained with them until November, when the Germans were defeated and forced to withdraw from Ukraine.

*S*oon after the German soldier's burial, Manya and
Israel felt a strange new tension between them. Israel
was becoming more and more eager to marry, but
there were obstacles to the union. Manya knew that marriage
at this time could not be considered. Yosel had twice denied
permission for Pavlusha to marry Ruchel because Pavlusha
was a Bolshevik, and Yosel had always been violently
opposed to the revolution. With Ruchel unwed, it was
unthinkable for Manya, her younger sister, to marry first.

Manya was a timid sweetheart, having been sheltered all
her life. Israel, on the other hand, had left home when he was
11 years old and had been on his own since then. Through the
years he had been in constant touch with his family, for as
the youngest brother he was much loved and worried about.
But he alone had been responsible for his daily welfare, and
this independence had matured him. Now he was ready for
marriage, and he was not willing to wait just so that a tradition could be upheld.

As a result, Manya was filled with private fears. She sensed
a restlessness in Israel and thought his ardor might cool if he
felt she was not fervently trying to persuade her father to
allow them to marry. The German's untimely death had

indeed thrown the jigsaw puzzle into an entirely different pattern. Everything was uncertain. Manya decided to talk to her father immediately about marrying Israel.

Yosel was confused. Things were happening so quickly that the pace left him wavering and insecure. War and violence threatened all around him. Why should he deny his children their chance for happiness when there might be so little time for happiness left? He thoroughly disapproved of Pavlusha, that Bolshevik who had helped to overturn the government and who would now be glad to bury the middle class in the name of starting things anew. But he did love Ruchel. And while her beauty and brilliance were not to be denied, Yosel knew what a temper and shallow disposition lay beneath the surface.

In these troubled times, perhaps it would be better for his girls to have husbands. Perhaps he should seriously reconsider giving his permission to Ruchel and Pavlusha. As for Manya and Israel—well, any father would consider such a match a genuine prize. This young man had a keen mind, a ready wit, good looks, and a good profession. The match between him and Manya was surely arranged in heaven! Well then, he would speak to Leah and they would review the entire dilemma.

Later that week, the announcements were made. Ruchel would be married on the third Sunday in May. One week later, Manya would also become a bride. Let no one say that Yosel Polevoi married off both daughters at once to save a few rubles. This was the public explanation for the arrangement, but Manya knew that her parents did not wish to rob Ruchel of her status as the first to marry. She was proud of her parents' sensitivity. Instinctively, they always acted well on their children's behalf.

The spring of 1918 was a season of plans and dreams. The

house was electric with preparations, and everyone felt joyful as the wedding days drew near.

The weddings became the social highlight of an otherwise bleak year. As many relatives as could manage to get to Talne came. Soldiers returning from the front occupied most of the trains, and passenger travel on these troop trains was very rare. Yet Israel's brother Samuel managed to come with his daughter by hitching a ride on the steps of one of the railroad cars. Samuel's wife, Fania, was pregnant and could not join them, but she sent a handmade linen tablecloth from her own trousseau as a token of her love. Other relatives came to Talne by horse and wagon or on foot.

Manya had worked so feverishly to prepare for Ruchel's wedding that she was not sure she could muster the energy needed for her own. But youth has its own untapped resources. When Manya went to meet Israel's family at the town square, she was in full control and radiant, captivating them all. Israel's mother, fondly called Moma Tzenia, was more than satisfied. Here indeed was a charming, attractive addition to her brood. After an evening with the entire Polevoi clan, she credited heaven for this match, just as Yosel had done.

Everyone had prepared something special for Manya's wedding. Bubba Brucha gave Manya the precious feather quilts that had been part of her own dowry. Still a member of the household and a friend, Zigmund prepared an eloquent toast for the bride and groom.

In the village, the cooking and baking had been going on for three days before the Sabbath. Under the able supervision of Bubba and Leah, every aunt and cousin known for culinary skill made a contribution.

The wedding took place on May 30, 1918. Manya, in her silk dress with its gilt embroidery, felt eager and confident as she prepared to embark on the most significant event of her life. Amid flowers and blessings, she and Israel were joined together under the *chuppah,* or ceremonial canopy. After Israel broke a glass underfoot to symbolize the destruction of the Temple and to remind them of past Jewish suffering, the couple exchanged vows and kissed. In the presence of their loved ones they became husband and wife. This was the last time they would all be together in joy and safety. Many guests attending that day would not live to see one another again. But no one yet suspected that, and nothing could mar the splendor of the ceremony or the *seudah* that followed.

Yosel was a perfect host, and also a generous father. He was proud of the dowries he had given his girls. Each daughter received a small chest filled with gold rubles. He presented Ruchel with a lovely house not too far from the family home—exactly what she had wanted. To Manya he gave the key to a fully stocked drugstore in Manistritch, a *shtetl* about a half-day's journey by train. Above the store he was having living quarters built, but as they would not be ready until the fall, he had arranged temporary rooms for the couple.

The newlywed Abramsons' summer was idyllic. Manya proved to be a great help in running the store in Manistritch. Israel often left her in charge when he went to Uman for supplies. The woman from whom they rented rooms found Manya to be a delightful young bride. She had nothing but praise for Manya's tidiness and willingness to learn about kitchen matters. By the time they moved into their own flat, Manya showed such skill that Israel jokingly remarked, "You think I'm smart to have a wife like Manya. If I were really clever, I'd have a dozen like her."

Israel felt that he was the most fortunate man on earth. In one fell swoop, he had become the owner of a prospering business and the husband of a woman whose true measure he was only beginning to understand. In September, his happiness increased with the realization that in eight months he and Manya would become parents. They immediately relayed the news to the Polevois in Talne, who were delighted. Ruchel had become pregnant on her honeymoon, so Leah and Yosel would become grandparents twice within one year.

Arrangements were made for Manya to come home in her eighth month to await the birth of the child in Talne. Israel would join her as soon as he had word of the birth. He promised to be there in time for the *brit milah* (should it be a boy) and to remain until Manya was able to travel.

That spring, about a month before the baby was to be born, Israel took Manya to the train station. She was excited, but her anticipation was shadowed by apprehension. She dreaded leaving now. She was enormous and clumsy, yet the prospect of being apart from her husband made her feel small and insignificant. The sense of confidence that she felt when she was with Israel faded when she was separated from him.

Then, too, there were ugly rumors that the Red Army, a ragtag assortment of Communist students and peasants, was clashing with the anti-Communist White Army, which was made up of czarist soldiers and others opposed to the Bolsheviks. The Russian civil war had not yet touched the area around Talne directly, but war in the *shtetl* was a grim possibility. In addition, the Ukrainian People's Republic, which had declared its independence from Russia in January 1918, was now determined to resist the Reds. This only compounded the potential for violence.

Manya felt that this was a bad time to go away. But to have the baby without her family, in a town of strangers, was unthinkable. With characteristic steadfastness, she pressed her fears to the back of her mind and refused to acknowledge them. She gathered her courage and left Israel with a brave smile on her face.

In Talne, the family reunion was joyful. No foreboding existed there. Ruchel's daughter, Meilya, was tiny and pink. The sisters took turns caring for her, though Leah wished neither of them would bother. She enjoyed this return to maternal responsibilities and kept devising duties to occupy her daughters so that she herself would have the pleasure of caring for the child. The two sisters, more companionable now than they had ever been in the past, were pleased to let their mother have her way.

One night Manya confided to Ruchel, "I wish my baby would decide to come so that I could see Israel soon! I always thought this house would seem like home to me, but it surely doesn't anymore. I miss Israel so much, I can hardly bear it." That night, her son obliged her and was born. He was a big child—10 pounds and 9 ounces. But the midwife was capable and all went well. The infant was named Valodya, after Israel's deceased father, Velvel. The proud family began to prepare for the *ben zokher,* the celebration of the birth of a son.

When Boorah went to the village square to order provisions for the celebration, he heard some disquieting news. Several regiments of the White Army were raiding the countryside, trying to rout the Red Army in the towns and villages. Anyone found helping the White Army was to be apprehended and sentenced to death by the Communists. Anyone caught helping the Red Army was immediately shot by the Whites. There was much death and destruction. There was no way of knowing if Talne would be one of the towns invaded, but as a precautionary measure the railway station was being guarded, as was the main road into town. Every other week, it seemed, the railway system was being commandeered. But by whom, it was never made clear. In a state of panic, Boorah returned home with such facts as he had.

Yosel listened intently to his son's evaluation of the situation. His face, drained of its color, looked old and worried. He had heard that some peasants in the Red Army had bothered Jewish families in other villages, demanding clean clothes and food. Worse than that, there were rumors that the Whites were raiding Jewish communities on the pretext of searching for Bolshevik sympathizers. Jews, regardless of their actual politics, were always being accused of having revolutionary sympathies. Yosel had not dared to imagine that their lives could be in danger. If the Whites were in the area, it was a possibility and he must be realistic. Yet he could not think clearly. He and Leah had not closed their eyes since Manya had gone into labor the day before.

The only thing to do now, he concluded, was to lock the doors and pray. A fearful chill permeated the air as he told the family of his apprehension. In mute resignation, they realized that they could not hide or run with Manya and baby Valodya upstairs.

Manya, however, was unaware of these dangers as she lay serenely in her bed. She was so pleased with her handsome child that she thought nothing of the trial she had just undergone. Other than a slight hint of exhaustion around the eyes, there was no weariness about her. In fact, she was stimulated by her accomplishment. She beamed at the thought of the *brit milah* and Israel's coming. It made her blood surge to her temples. She called to her father expectantly, "Papa, Papa, have you sent word to Israel already? Is everything arranged for the *ben zokher*?"

When Yosel entered the room looking so ashen and worried, she didn't understand. "Father, aren't you well?" she asked. "Tell me what's wrong!"

"Manya, please listen carefully," he said. "I want you to understand everything clearly. There is a rumor that we will be invaded by the White Army. They are marauding all over the countryside, and they may come here. If we don't cooperate with them, we will surely pay a dear price. We'll let them have anything they wish, God help us, in exchange for our lives. So please, no hysterics. That can only cause us harm. I'm sorry, but there was no way to get a message out to Israel. We'll have to have the *bris* without him. But don't worry, we'll have it—so long as we are alive."

Manya looked at her father apprehensively, but Yosel soothed her with a reassuring smile. She settled against the feather pillows, comforted by his wisdom and his love. The very next day, she would be separated from him.

*T*he worst rumors of violence were all too soon con-
firmed for the Jews of Talne. Without warning, a White
Army battalion descended upon the village that next
morning like a flock of vultures. With frightening speed, the
cold-eyed soldiers went from house to house, searching out
every man and boy above the age of 12. Apparently, they
were making sure that the Red Army could not enlist these
men and boys to swell their own ranks. The Jews were sin-
gled out for special persecution. The entire Jewish male population, including Yosel and his two sons, was taken to an
open field at the edge of town. There, they were ordered to
line up in the overgrown clearing and to stand at attention.

In the *shtetl*, terror gripped those who were left behind.
The isolated women of the Polevoi household were petrified
with fear. They kept occupied with their routine chores to
avoid thinking about their men, yet they could not ignore the
terrible possibility that they would never see Yosel, Boorah,
and little Mikhail again. And what about Pavlusha? He was
not at home, yet they worried about him, too. Who could tell

what dangers he would face? The Whites took special delight in capturing and killing Communists.

At midday Yosel's sister D'vora and his sister-in-law Pearl came to the side doors, shrieking and sobbing. The Polevois quickly let them in and bolted the doors behind their hysterical relatives. The women sobbed out their horrifying story. The White Guard had broken into their home, searching for any hidden males who had not surrendered in the morning roundup. When Pearl's oldest child, 14-year-old Boris, had been discovered, he had been instantly shot under the bed where he crouched. As Pearl had let out an uncontrollable scream and had run to help the child who lay moaning in a pool of blood, she had been knocked unconscious and raped in front of her fatally injured son. And that was not the end of it. Through desperate tears, the women told of stopping off at their sister Hoodi's home, only to find that tragedy had already struck there, too. Because Hoodi's husband was known to be well-to-do and because their home was expensively furnished, the beasts who broke in had insisted that there was more gold there than they had first taken. When no more could be uncovered, one helmeted maniac known as "Big Stanislav" had grabbed the women in the house, had lined them up against a wall, and had forced his fingers into their vaginas, claiming to look for gold coins. One of the girls had just started her monthly period, and he had killed her for soiling his hands.

As the tragic story unfolded, blind terror marked the faces of the listeners. They stood, chalk-white, unable even to offer sympathy, so shocked were they. In the presence of her speechless relatives, Pearl began to beat her breasts and pull out her hair by the roots. Only a glass of vodka calmed her. Finally, battling to regain some composure, Pearl and D'vora prayed that God would be with them, for they were going from door to door to warn the other townspeople. Leah, realizing that her sisters-in-law were crazed with grief, begged them both to remain. But the women could not be persuaded. After drinking a second glass of vodka and taking the food that Leah insisted on giving them, they left on their fruitless mission of mercy.

Two hours passed and all was quiet. Leah could only pray for her men and beseech God to spare her house. Suddenly, someone was pounding on the front door. Bubba, who had lived through other pogroms, froze at the sound. Her first instinct was not to answer it. But she knew that if she didn't respond, the soldiers would riddle the house with bullets, break the windows, and gain access anyway. So she cautiously answered the door. Outside stood four soldiers. Before they could push their way inside, she barred the entrance with her body and invited them in. By performing this useless gesture, she felt she did not give up all control.

The soldiers told her that they were looking for hidden men and valuables. To this, Bubba said matter-of-factly, "Help yourself—look where you like." Then she added, "One request: we are only women and babies here. Do what you will with me, but please spare the others any indignities. You will surely be rewarded by God, and Jesus will smile on you."

At this unexpected comment, one soldier's face softened—but only for an instant. Then he and the others started to search the place.

Leah came into the room with a start. She had been busy with Manya and Valodya upstairs and had not heard the commotion at the door. Silently, she followed the soldiers from room to room, watching as they tore at some things and overturned others, taking treasures that had been accumulated over a lifetime. The family had not hidden anything, because they reasoned that if the soldiers found enough to satisfy them, they would spare their lives. Some soldiers with twisted minds enjoyed making a well-to-do Jew destitute as much as they enjoyed killing him.

"Who needs it anyway? I just hope they leave us with our lives," Leah told herself.

When they were finished ransacking the first floor, the soldiers went upstairs. One soldier, noticing that Leah and Bubba seemed agitated, accelerated his pace. He sensed that there might be a windfall in one of the bedrooms.

The men searched room after room, ordering Ruchel to lead them. She did this with Meilya in her arms, too frightened to let go of the child for an instant. Finally, with much hesitation, she took the soldiers to Manya's bedroom and told Manya what they were after.

Manya whispered, "Look wherever you like," and protectively drew her son closer to her bosom. When a thorough search produced nothing more of value, the soldiers rounded up all of the women and put them into the room with Manya and Valodya.

One of the soldiers snarled, "If you want to leave this room alive, show us where more gold is hidden."

In truth, the women had no more and pleaded with their captors to believe them.

"Well then," asked the biggest soldier, "why did you all seem so upset when we came into this room?"

"Only because my daughter has had the child so recently— just three days ago. Please . . ."

But as Leah spoke, the same soldier, a brute with a twitchy mustache, rushed forward and threw back the covers of Manya's bed, demanding that she get out of the bed so that it could be thoroughly searched. Haltingly, Manya tried to comply. She gingerly lowered one leg and then another. She had been badly torn during delivery, and now as she stood upright, the pain smarted bitterly. She turned around to reach for her son, but the sadistic soldier grabbed the tiny creature and threw him hard onto the adjacent bed. The startled baby bellowed, and the anguished grandmothers rushed forward to defend their children. The soldier coolly turned and struck Leah with the butt of his rifle, commanding that she leave the room. She refused, fearing that the others might be harmed in her absence. At this, two of the soldiers grabbed her roughly and dragged her, screaming, out of the room. Ruchel and Manya listened in mute hysteria to the sound of Leah's body being lugged up the stairs toward the attic. Channa and Bubba clung to each other and sobbed without restraint. The soldiers finally subdued the old grandmother and bound and gagged her. Then the soldiers who remained in the room continued their treasure hunt but found nothing.

Suddenly the air was punctuated by a clear, ringing shot.

"Oh my God, they've killed our mother!" screamed Ruchel.

Manya shrieked, "Mother, Mother, Mother," over and over, in uncontrollable panic. Only a slap that drew blood silenced her.

The terrified women stayed in that room for at least an hour. The babies cried, but their mothers were not permitted to touch them. Through all this, Channa was whimpering, certain that she or any of them might also be killed, now that Mama was gone. Oh God. Mama.

Suddenly, a fifth soldier appeared. He did not seem to know any of the other four. Yet after he muttered something to them, they immediately gathered up their booty and vanished.

At first, the women stood immobile with shock from their ordeal. Ruchel, who recovered first, ran immediately to the attic, hoping desperately that the shot had not been fatal and that perhaps Leah was still alive. When she entered, she found her mother sitting in a chair, disheveled and staring vacantly ahead of her, but obviously very much alive.

"Mama!" Ruchel cried. "We heard a gun go off and thought they had shot you!"

She sobbed in utter relief. Leah's swollen face was still expressionless.

She replied, "I'm surprised they didn't," and hoarsely she added, "I guess they wanted you to think that—those barbarians. Is everyone alive down there?"

Ruchel dried her eyes and said, "Fine—we are all fine. Mama, did they hurt you very much?"

She caressed her mother tenderly. Leah's eyes flashed with pain, but she simply swallowed, straightened her clothes, and left the room. She said nothing. Whatever indignities she had suffered would remain unknown. She would not add to her family's grief by telling them what had happened. She volunteered no details, and her children loved her too much to even dare speculate.

Bubba went silently into the kitchen to fix food for Meilya and the rest of them. Somehow they would have to survive. Alone and bruised, with no news of their men, they could only wait and hope for Pavlusha's return.

Israel Polevoi (Yosel's brother) stands behind brother Yankel, his wife, Pearl, and their sons, Mikhail, Simon, and Boris. Boris (far right) was killed by the White Guard during the pogrom of May 1919.

Above: *Yosel's sister Hoodi* (right), *her husband, and their daughter Manya. Manya also lost her life during the 1919 pogrom.*

Below: *Yosel's sister D'vora and her daughters*

58

*M*eanwhile, the men and boys who had been rounded up that morning had been marched to a meadow for execution. From the time they had been routed from their homes, they had been ordered to maintain silence. When they had reached the open field at the edge of town, they had been lined up and told to stand with their hands clasping the backs of their necks. Some of the men had tried to escape to the nearby woods, but they had all been captured. So there they stood, unable to escape, facing a platoon of soldiers and several machine guns. Apparently, the soldiers were just waiting for a signal to mow their captives down. As it became clear that the end was near, the more religious Jews began to pray. The suffering of all the men was made more acute by their worrying about the fate of their families. The men were careful to obey every command, hoping that if they cooperated, at least the women and children left behind might be spared.

The soldiers itched to get on with it. Both they and the prisoners had been standing there for hours, and the sun that beat down on them was scorching. The prisoners were not allowed to move. Those who could not control their bodily functions soiled themselves. Others grimaced with the pain that comes from perseverance. As the day wore on, some men and young boys fell from heat exhaustion. One man went mad and had to be restrained. Why didn't the soldiers just kill them? What futility! Some took the wait to be a good omen. Others thought it was useless to hope when doom was so obviously at hand. They could do nothing but accept their destiny.

The soldiers were becoming increasingly impatient. They complained to their platoon leader, who told them that he could not give them the order to shoot until he himself received the command.

"After all," he lectured, "this is not a Jew or two, but a whole town. Hundreds of them. Why should I take the responsibility without the proper authority? I was ordered to wait for the command, and that order was signed by the commander in chief of the Russian Southwestern Armies, Anton Ivanovitch Denikin, himself. So I shall wait. Do I need the whole White Army on my head?"

And so they stayed, hour after hour. As the prisoners fidgeted in place, Yosel began to daydream. With his life on earth coming to an end, he reviewed all its highlights. One by one, he recalled the incidents that had given him joy and made him proud. His chest grew so tight with emotion that he could hardly draw a breath.

Suddenly his thoughts returned to 1912. It was a good year—a very good year. It was the year when he and Benuman Mogilev had been elected *gaboyim* (leaders) of the local *besmedresh*. He relived the entire celebration of his election. On that warm spring day, in honor of the occasion, he and Mogilev had presented the congregation with two handsome Torahs. They were decorated with jewels and had exquisitely designed silver torah crowns. Beneath the silver breastplates hung small tags that permanently identified the donors.

With Torahs in hand, he and Mogilev had walked under a canopy carried by their children, leading a parade of the entire congregation and their families through the streets of Talne. Musicians with fiddles had accompanied the procession. Tears stuck in Yosel's throat as he remembered. Leah had prepared the most magnificent feast the town had ever known, and all were invited—from intimate friends to mere acquaintances. Even some strangers had accepted the open invitation for a good meal, for it had truly been a *mitzvah* to celebrate the presentation of sanctified gifts.

Thoughts of Leah made him break down. Now he saw her in his arms, crying bitterly about his plans to make a business trip to America. It could have been a journey which, if successful, would have made him an internationally wealthy trader. Yosel had seen that all horizons were shrinking and that world travel was becoming routine. Yet his going would have required an absence of about two years. Leah had found this unbearable. Her tears had weakened his resolve. After all, he had decided, money was a foolish partner for a cold winter's night. His mother, too, had approved of his decision not to go abroad. He recalled her wisely remarking, "After all, Yosel, *challah* may be the staff of life, but if you try to swallow a whole loaf at once, you'll very likely choke."

And in truth, he was well enough fixed for the life of a *shtetl* Jew. Though it would have been a great adventure to go to America, it could be no substitute for his present contentment.

Abruptly, Yosel's pleasant memories were interrupted. From the corner of the field came a rider. He whispered a message to the platoon leader and rode away. The sun was setting. Although some of the men had fainted, most of the prisoners in the field were still standing. The platoon leader went over to his men, who were gathered in small groups, and spoke to them briefly. Silently, they packed up their weapons and left the field.

Could it be? After several moments of remaining at attention, the men moved uncertainly from their assigned positions. They had been spared! It was almost too much to believe! They were totally bewildered and could only accept their release as a miracle from God. Perhaps it had been a test of their faith—a trial by ordeal. Later they would learn that the Red Army had struck in force. They had amassed a huge following and had chased the White Army from every town and village in that part of the countryside.

Stiff and weak, the men slowly began to walk home. Soon, their paces quickened to a run. When Yosel and Boorah came home with Mikhail trailing behind them, and it was plain that everyone was alive, there was wild rejoicing. It seemed unbelievable that the whole family had been spared. But after seeing the damage done to his house and hearing what had happened to his family and relatives, Yosel could eat little of the meal that had been prepared for him. He picked at the food. Boorah and Mikhail, too, were sickened by the tales of what had happened to some of the women.

Following the terrible *sachud*—the reign of terror—there was a lingering uneasiness. The violence had ended, but it could come again. So after the men returned, they agreed it would be wise for the family to hide in the root cellar for a few days. The house had been thoroughly ransacked, and nothing of value remained. If the Whites returned, they would find a seemingly abandoned dwelling.

When Valodya was eight days old, all preparations were in order for the *bris,* or circumcision. The family decided that the ritual would be performed in the safety of the root cellar. That way, if there were any sudden intruders, they could go right on with the ceremony. On the day of the *bris,* the *mohel* and *sandek* were called in, and the family was assembled in the cellar. The child was brought to the center of the room. Quickly, with skill and precision, the *mohel* completed the circumcision. There was a hasty *Kiddush,* and the infant was officially welcomed into the Covenant of Abraham. That night and for several more, the family slept in their underground sanctuary.

Gradually, as time passed and no new fighting occurred in the area, the Polevois began to relax a little. By mid-July, the situation in Talne was much more stable. The lazy summer sun melted people's anxieties away, and slowly the village returned to normal. It seemed as if the Whites had forgotten about Talne and were not planning to return, so people began to perform their routine duties without hesitation. Only those who had lost loved ones still mourned. The others took up their lives where they had been interrupted.

Although the railway system had broken down, once in a while a train did arrive. Manya decided to take Valodya and return to Manistritch. She had not seen or heard from Israel for three months, and she was sick with worry about him, fearing that there might have been trouble in Manistritch as well as in Talne. Manya's parents tried to reason with her. They begged her to leave the infant with them if she insisted on wandering off alone without knowing what she would find. Manya, however, was adamant. Valodya was two months old now, and the time had come for her to leave— with him. She would not consider leaving her son behind.

She stayed with Valodya at the train station day and night, waiting for a train to appear. Each day a member of the family came and brought food and stayed with them. When a train finally arrived, Yosel and Leah were both there. They clung to the baby, smothering him with hugs and kisses. But they did not let their daughter sense how deeply they feared for her and for Valodya. They were truly afraid that the pair might not reach Israel alive. These times were too uncertain, too troubled. The fact that Israel himself had not made contact with them seemed ominous. But Manya was too involved with thoughts of seeing her husband again to feel their apprehensions. Her vigil had ended, and she was ready to go.

Yosel helped Manya board the train and placed her bundles beside the basket with the child. He and Leah bid her Godspeed, but just as the flatcar began to pull away, they heard their names being called frantically. In astonishment, they saw that Israel was on a boxcar pulling into the station on an adjacent track!

They could only shout, "Manya!" and point.

Israel did not lose a moment. He jumped directly from the still-moving boxcar to the flatcar, and clasped the astonished Manya in a triumphant embrace. Leah and Yosel watched their children standing on the flatcar and clinging to each other until the train had chugged away out of sight. When Leah's vision blurred, she could not be sure if it was because of the distance or her free-flowing tears.

When Israel finally looked at the child, sleeping peacefully in the basket, he asked, "God in heaven, is it a boy or a girl?"

Only then did the full impact of the situation hit Manya.

"Good God," she thought, "He doesn't know! He doesn't know he has a son!"

She lifted the drowsy Valodya into Israel's eager arms, and he held his son until, at last, they reached Manistritch. Only when they were in their home did he finally lay the baby down to embrace his wife. It had been more than three months since they had been together. With no word, the last two months had been torturous.

*F*or weeks afterwards Manya and Israel talked, overwhelmed, of their miraculous meeting, of the miracle
of the baby, and of the miracle of their being alive.
But behind the euphoria of the reunion lingered persistent
memories of their recent trials. Manya recounted the brutal
trauma in Talne. Over and over she painfully recalled the
episode. She tried to purge herself by detailing everything—
everything, that is, except her mother's ordeal. This she
could not bring herself to reveal. It was not that she thought
she could block out the memory with her silence. Rather, she
felt duty-bound not to discuss her mother's experience, even
though she knew that Israel would be understanding.

For his part, Israel told of having tried to reach Talne
about two months earlier. It had been time for the baby's
birth, and in the absence of any word he had decided to take
a chance and come anyway. At worst, he had thought, it
would mean an extra few day's to a week's wait. On the way,
a White Army platoon had stopped his train, robbed him,
and beaten him mercilessly. He told Manya how one soldier
had splintered his glasses against his face with his booted
foot, and how another had cut his body with silver spurs.
Gravely injured and unconscious, he had been left to die.

But a gentle old dog had passed by and licked his wounds. When the dog's master had come to retrieve it, he had found Israel, wretched and feverish, and had taken pity on him. He had put Israel in a cart, had taken him to his own home, and had compassionately nursed him back to health. Only when the swelling and discoloration in Israel's face had finally subsided and his other wounds were healed had he attempted another trip to Talne.

Manya listened, horrified, as he told his tale. She shivered with fear at the realization that Israel had almost been taken from her. In the days that followed, they tried to return to a normal existence. Old friends congregated to toast their health as new parents. Jews and gentiles alike—all who wished the Abramsons well—were invited to their home. But diluting each moment of joy was a nagging remembrance. Time— they both depended so much on time to help them forget and to help them return to life's former rhythm. And after a while, their life did begin to settle down again.

Most of the war activity now seemed far removed from Manistritch. But elsewhere in Ukraine, the fighting between the Red and White armies still continued. A third army— that of the Ukrainian nationalists, under the leadership of Simon Petlura—now complicated the war. They were fighting to safeguard Ukraine's recently established independence from Lenin's central Communist government. For the moment, however, these conflicts seemed confined to the big cities. Having heard no news for a considerable time, the Jews of Manistritch became beguiled by their own hopes, and their anxieties were lulled by the hot summer nights.

When the Red Army did ride into town in mid-August, they found a sleepy village where people conducted their daily affairs in peace, oblivious to the political upheaval surrounding them. After the Communists quartered themselves, they set out on skirmishes to intercept platoons of anti-Communists, who were creating havoc in the local villages and towns. Though the Communists seemed to have no interest in bothering the local citizens, no one in Manistritch knew exactly what all the activity implied, and most were too intimidated to find out.

Like her father, Manya was opposed to Lenin's Russian Communist government. Yosel felt that there was much greater hope for the Jewish middle class under the newly formed Ukrainian People's Republic. The reforms it had enacted seemed to prove that a new era of political recognition was beginning for the Jews. They, among other minorities within Ukraine, had just been guaranteed full rights by the new government. Yosel felt that his economic rights, as well as his political ones, would be better honored by the Ukrainian government than by the Russian Communist party. Yet he, like most Jews, had always considered himself to be Russian. He had no affinity for the Ukrainian culture and remembered with fear and suspicion the many anti-Semitic excesses of the Ukrainians. Despite this, he was inclined to support the Ukrainians out of political and economic considerations.

Yosel's heated discussions on this subject had made a strong impression on Manya, and she feared the threat of the Communist takeover keenly. She treasured Israel's position in the community, the financial security of the drugstore, and the comfort of their home. She knew that Lenin's Communist government would not especially benefit them. She could not imagine that the Communists would make things better for Jews in general, either. Israel often said that the Jews most active in the Bolshevik movement were people who had little interest in Jewish traditions. They seemed willing to abandon them for the alluring promise of a lighter yoke.

Although people like Israel and Manya had their opinions

about the conflict, their life in Manistritch was not yet directly affected by it. Since the armistice with Germany, life in Manistritch was uneventful, and autumn passed quietly. Soon, the Christmas season arrived. Manya and Israel were invited to join the holiday celebrations of their friends the Bernatovitches, a Christian couple who owned the sausage plant in town. The plant was quite close to Israel's drugstore, and the two couples had become fast friends. The Abramsons felt quite comfortable with these *goyim:* Manya felt so secure in her Jewishness that she welcomed the opportunity to talk about her beliefs. The Bernatovitches, in turn, were a charming couple who appreciated the Abramsons' wit and congeniality.

The Christmas Eve party was splendid. The Bernatovitch home was large and impressively furnished, and all guests were warmly welcomed. Since childhood, Israel and Manya had each watched the caroling and festivities of Christmas as outsiders. This was the first time that they had actually been part of the celebration, and they thoroughly enjoyed it. Throughout the evening, the conversation was stimulating and the refreshments were abundant. The guests ate dried fruits and cheese and drank a great deal of wine and schnapps. The merriment lasted for hours, and by the time the evening had ended the Abramsons were very giddy.

After lingering goodbyes, they walked home laughing and swaying, too intoxicated to notice the wooden fence on which was scrawled, "Kill the Jews and Save Russia." Unknown to the Jews of Manistritch, anti-Jewish slogans were springing up all over the countryside. The slogans were part of an intensifying campaign to blame the Jews for the country's troubles. Slowly, the net was closing around them.

On Christmas Day, a man brought news that so far all was quiet in Talne. But he said that although everyone thought that the villages would be spared further involvement in the fighting, the conflict was growing more intense. Many people believed that the Red Army was winning, and they feared a final takeover by the Communist party. But he personally thought that if the Communists held power in Russia it would improve matters for the Ukrainian Jews.

Israel shifted uneasily as he listened. He did not agree with the man and was glad that he had buried his gold behind the house. He was beginning to feel a definite threat to himself and to other Jews. He judged the man to be naive, and after the fellow left he decided to take further precautions.

"It's better to be overprepared than to be mourned," he told Manya. "Put a few things in a sack for Bernatovitch to hold for us. In spite of what our friend just said, we might have to leave this place in a big hurry."

Manya agreed and did so at once. After her bitter experiences in Talne, she knew that a sudden pogrom was not beyond the realm of possibility. The good Madame Bernatovitch offered whatever help she could give them in an emergency, fully aware that she might have to give it under penalty of death. Even in those black days, people of good will and reason still resisted cruelty and injustice.

The atmosphere in Manistritch began to grow tense. That week, contradictory rumors passed from one end of town to the other. There was a humming network of information, but the facts changed hourly. No one seemed to be truly informed. Only one thing was certain—a momentum was building. Then the town heard from a "reliable source" that in many parts of Ukraine where the Red Army was overwhelming the Ukrainian forces, the Ukrainians were going berserk. As their hope for maintaining independence faded, they were expressing their fury and disillusionment by reverting to the age-old outlet—pogroms. Whole *shtetls* were being burned, and the Ukrainian leader Petlura was standing by while thousands of Jews were being massacred by his men.

Although the Ukrainian army was rumored to be moving in the opposite direction from Manistritch, the Jews still felt the threat of a pogrom. Several of the Abramsons' friends made plans to leave the country. Some hoped to get to Palestine. Others planned to get to Romania (they had arranged it for a price), and from there to Belgium or England. Others would try to reach American shores by whatever route they could. Some had family elsewhere in Europe and said they would try to contact them. These were all affluent businesspeople, part of the remaining minority of middle-class Jews who still had financial means. They accepted dispersal as the only means of survival.

The Abramsons, however, would not entertain the thought of leaving. For Israel, there was still the dream of a life of "milk and honey" as part of the Polevoi family. He could not wrest himself from such luxury and coveted status. Like his father-in-law, he felt that his hidden resources would see them through. Manya, who had always been close to her family, could not conceive of life permanently separated from her parents. Of course, she did have relatives in the United States. Her aunt and uncle, Raisel and Frank Olson (Olschanetzki), and her uncle Israel Polevoi were prospering there. Israel, too, had a brother, Benjamin, a doctor in North Carolina, another brother, Herman, in Pennsylvania, and three sisters—Sophia, Sarah, and Miriam—in New York. It was comforting to know that should they have to emigrate, there were lifelines.

New Year's Eve, 1920, fell on a Friday, and it should have been a busy day for Israel. But business in general had ground to a halt, partly because of a heavy snowfall and partly because the *goyim* were getting an early start on their celebrating. This afforded Israel the perfect excuse to spend the day relaxing upstairs with Manya and Valodya. It was a warm, cozy afternoon. The samovar was hot, and Manya's cooking and baking produced a blend of aromas that was intoxicating. Valodya had been put in his crib early so that Manya and Israel could get ready for a few Sabbath guests who had also chosen to remain in Manistritch.

Marina, a local Christian peasant girl, had come as usual to help Manya prepare for the Sabbath. She always lavished affection on Valodya and gave Manya efficient help with the chores. As she and Manya worked together in the kitchen, Manya mused, "Shabbos really regenerates the spirit, especially in troubled times. It's hard to believe that before the Hebrew people developed the Sabbath, people and animals were expected to work until they dropped of exhaustion. It's a revolutionary idea in the history of mankind—that all living things are entitled to a day of rest." Marina smiled, and Israel nodded in agreement. The Abramsons never wavered in their belief that the Sabbath was truly a God-inspired tradition. Whatever tensions, defeats, or agonies a week held, the Sabbath lifted the soul. It was dreamed about all week and savored when it finally arrived.

That evening was memorable, for Manya was an excellent hostess. At her gatherings the guest list and the menu always varied, but not the hospitality. Each Sabbath Israel would declare that it was the best, and that night was no exception. Manya beamed.

Then, as she and Marina were clearing the table after the last neighbor had left. there was a soft knock at the door. It was Kushner from the dry goods store down the street. Something was terribly wrong. His whole body was shaking as he entered the room, and his face was dead white. In a choked, halting voice, he told a terrible story. Apparently, his cousin's entire family had just been bizarrely murdered by Ukrainian soldiers. Following his own Sabbath meal, he had gone to pay them a visit and had walked in to find bloodied human remains scattered throughout the house—heads in some rooms, bodies, arms, and legs in others. His voice was trembling, but he was coherent. He had come back to the store to get money from his secret depository, and when he had seen the Abramsons' lights on he had come over, desperately needing to talk to someone. He wept unabashedly. He was going to escape right away. It was clear that the Jews of Manistritch were about to face the horror of a pogrom once again.

*G*lued to their places, the Abramsons listened to Kushner's story in terror. Israel began to perspire and felt his hands become clammy. Manya's heart pounded wildly in her chest as she made a package of food for Kushner before he went on his way.

They had never been more frightened. Yet they preferred the safety of their home to the cold, dark night outside. They reasoned that often during pogroms whole houses were spared. while others were entirely wiped out. Had it not been so in Talne less than one year ago? Although it was against Sabbath customs to do so, they carefully darkened the house to minimize the threat of intrusion. Then they got into bed with all of their clothing on and lay there listening for sounds through the howling winds, their temples pounding and their bodies in a cold sweat. Not a word was spoken—there was nothing to say. In their silent prayers, they asked that the shadows of night protect them.

Several hours later, sometime after midnight, the sound of breaking glass split the air. There was an insistent banging on the bolted door. Soldiers were shouting demands to be let in.

"This is it!" Israel yelled. "Grab Valodya and run like hell. Stay right behind me!"

And so they fled through the back door, fugitives vainly hoping to disappear in the darkness. For several blocks Manya kept to Israel's heels until she had to swerve to avoid being hit by a horse-drawn carriage. When she regained her balance, Israel was nowhere in sight! Manya stopped to consider what to do. The logical place to run would be to Madame Bernatovitch's. But Manya recalled that her friend was spending New Year's Eve with her sister in a nearby village. Knowing that the Bernatovitches would not be home, Manya considered several alternatives in the space of a few seconds and finally decided to run to the synagogue. Surely, once Israel realized that she was not behind him, he too, would pick the synagogue as the most logical place to meet. Fortunately, it was only a few blocks away.

Israel, meanwhile, had run several blocks before he missed Manya. For a moment he was stupefied. Then he thought of the bundle he had told Manya to leave with Madame Bernatovitch. Despite the distance, he decided that Manya had probably gone to the Bernatovitches' home. He did not know that the couple were not there, and so he began to run faster. Even his limp did not slow him down.

Manya, meanwhile, ran past streets strangely bright with angry orange flames. "Oh God," she begged, "please don't let the synagogue be burned, too!"

Now she could see nothing through the thick smoke except the flash of flames leaping to the sky. Here and there tortured shrieks filled the blackness. There was the sound of a child sobbing close by. As Manya pushed on, the sobbing became louder. Suddenly, through smoke, she saw the burning silhouette of a small boy. Manya laid her bundled baby in the snow, grabbed the child, and rolled him over and over, extinguishing the flames. He was now weeping hysterically, clinging to her. She drew him to her bosom, kissed his head, and spoke softly in an effort to comfort him. At the same time, she looked nervously around her for signs of any more soldiers, although it was obvious that there was nothing left to destroy on this street.

When Manya asked the child where his mother was, he led her to a charred body, but the woman was beyond help. Fear gripped Manya. She had to get to the synagogue. Israel must be there! She unhinged the boy's hands from her skirt and started to leave, telling the child to stay near his house so that one of his family might find him in the morning. She assured him that his father would return, although the boy had no idea of his whereabouts.

"Take me with you," the child begged. "I'll be another son to you. You will see how good I am—and capable. I'll be a big help to you. I'll mind your baby. Please, I beg of you, don't leave me alone! I'm so scared!"

Again he grabbed the hem of her skirt. He would not let her free. Manya's heart was torn.

"Angel, child, I wish I could take you," she cried, "But I have no place to go. I have no place for you, nor one for myself!"

Manya knew the child was badly injured and in pain. No doubt his burns would blister and become infected if left untreated. But taking him would slow her down. It would mean risking Valodya's chances for survival. This risk she could not take.

"You must stay here where you can be found and cared for by your family. Surely one of your relations will find you in the morning," she said desperately.

She wrenched her skirt away, leaving some cloth in the boy's tiny hand, picked up Valodya, and ran.

He called after her, "Mama, Mama, don't go! Please don't go!" Manya felt her knees buckle and thought she would faint. Only her determination to get Valodya to safety sustained her.

God in Heaven, the synagogue was left untouched! Inside she leaned gratefully against a carved pillar and caught her breath. Suddenly. she saw a ladder standing before her begin to move upward. The Jews already hiding in the attic were removing the ladder, to prevent the soldiers from claiming more victims. Impulsively, she grabbed the bottom rung and forced it down.

Climbing up slowly, she shouted, "Would you have a woman and child risk death below while you are safe up there?" But no one answered. Once in the attic, she looked all over for Israel, but he was not among the 30-or-so people who had taken refuge here. She was desolate. There was nothing to do but wait. She settled herself in a spot from which she could see the large front doors and glanced around at her fellow survivors. Some were bloodied and some were burned; all were thankful to be alive. The man who had lifted the ladder closed the attic door softly. Soon the room was filled with rhythmical breathing of sleeping people.

Manya looked from one face to another. Everyone seemed to he asleep but her. Even Valodya was warm now and he slept without a peep. Quietly, she wept.

A man to her right whispered, "Don't worry—the worst is probably over. You'll have quite a tale to tell the baby's children."

Manya knew he meant to comfort her. She supposed he thought she was crying because of her predicament—and well she could have been. But her tears were not for herself. She cried for the pitiful child she had left behind. She felt stinging pangs of guilt and shame. Alone with the knowledge of what she had done, she did not rationalize. She could not justify her actions, and she knew her retribution would be remembrance. From that moment on, through the rest of her life, she would be plagued by the sin she had committed this night. She vowed never to tell it to anyone. This one deed she would carry, unrevealed, to her grave. While the others slept, she sobbed.

Sometime during the night, Manya finally dozed off into a fitful sleep. But abruptly, she was awakened by a violent crash as the synagogue doors flew open below.

In they poured! It sounded like a full detachment. Petlura's soldiers barged into the sanctuary, tore out the pews, and defiled the Torahs, spreading them all over the floor. As a final act of desecration, they used the synagogue as a stable for their horses. Now everyone in the attic was awake, trembling. They listened as the soldiers sang, drank, laughed and finally slept. The tension in the air was thicker than the acrid smoke from the smoldering buildings outside. No one stirred; all breathing seemed imprisoned. Manya snuggled Valodya to her bosom, ready to stifle any murmur. But Valodya slept soundly.

At dawn, the soldiers rose and prepared to leave. They saddled their horses and spoke of looking elsewhere in town for more Jews and Red Army soldiers. As the last horse galloped away, cheers of relief broke out in the attic. Looking out of the window, the survivors could see only the charred remains of buildings. Petlura's bandits could do no more damage to this part of the town.

The man who had raised the ladder and closed the door now reopened it to lower the ladder. As he unlatched the door and swung it open, thick smoke rose into the attic.

"*Vey-iz-meer!*" cried one of the men. "They must have lit the straw before they left."

Pandemonium broke loose. The single window in the attic

was smashed, and the ladder lowered to a ledge. Those trapped inside now reasoned that from this ledge, they could jump to the ground and perhaps escape with minor sprains or injuries. Manya got in line with the rest of them, waiting her turn to crawl through the window. As she waited, the flames licked the attic floor and the heat became scorching. She truly believed that she and Valodya had come to their end, and that they would now be burned alive. Her skin began to crawl.

When the room became too hot to bear, the entire group crowded on the upper precipice outside, waiting their turn to go down the ladder to the lower ledge.

Suddenly, one of the men said coarsely. "Madame, you were the last to come up, you'll be the last to go down. Anyway, going down with a baby will slow us all up."

Valodya wailed angrily as if to rebuke him. Manya, coughing and nauseous from the smoke, offered no resistance and gave up her place in line. She had no choice. As she circled around, there was not one sympathetic glance. Here, survival instincts ruled. As she retreated to the end of the line, Manya saw flames inside the window and realized that to wait for her turn would be fatal. If they weren't cremated, she and Valodya would die of smoke inhalation. She would have to act. While the others, still waiting for the ladder, watched her, she encircled her baby as best she could with her own body—and jumped.

She fell hard. Valodya's shrieks knifed the air. Manya's head reeled, and it was some seconds before she composed herself. As she frantically gathered up her baby, she saw that the snow beneath him was red with blood.

Unbelieving, she touched the snow. It was hard as rock. Frozen mud and ice lay beneath the fresh snowfall. She removed Valodya's cap, now stained scarlet, and saw a jagged gash in his scalp from his crown to the nape of his neck. Although she was in shock, she managed to tear a rag from her slip and bandage his bleeding wound. Valodya's small body quivered, and he screamed convulsively.

Manya told herself over and over that her baby would live, if only she could reach Madame Bernatovitch. If God was with her, the Bernatovitches would be home, and surely they'd help her. She prayed that they would remember the promise they had made in a more carefree time. Now, they were her only realistic hope. She ran wildly in the direction of their home with only one thought in mind: to get help for Valodya.

She knew she must not go directly to a doctor. Who would help a dying Jewish infant at the risk of his own life? And no doubt the doctors were being carefully watched. No, she had to get help from the Bernatovitches. She would have to get across town or Valodya would die. He was already still and blue, and his breathing was raspy. She ran for his life, and was only three blocks from her destination when a soldier on a stallion commanded her to halt. As he rode up to her, she suddenly stopped, transfixed.

"Where are you going, Jewess?" he asked, and without pausing, added, "Are you crazy running through the streets? Don't you see what's happening all over town?"

With determination she replied, "My baby's had an accident; you can see the blood for yourself. I'm taking him to a doctor. Please let me pass. You see I'm in a hurry—and I'm sorry to disappoint you, but I'm no Jew. Here, I'll prove it."

Manya was eyeing an old peasant lady walking behind the soldier.

"Come here," she called. "My baby's hurt and I'm on my way to the doctor. Tell this soldier you know who I am and that I'm no Jew!"

Manya turned so that the soldier could not see the pleading expression on her face. The peasant woman was frightened to death. But she was overcome with pity, too, at the sight of the crimson slip. Unwilling to endanger her own life with a lie, she hedged.

"She's not really familiar. She's not from this neighborhood, but I do think I see her sometimes in church. Yes, I recall seeing her at mass a few times." This was as much as she was willing to say before she scurried off.

The soldier laughed down at Manya. "You're brave, dammit, and smart. Get out of here before you get yourself killed."

With that, he withdrew his glistening saber from its sheath and struck Manya fiercely with the dull edge of the blade. The impact sent her spinning in the snow. Valodya tumbled down, too, and rolled a short distance away.

Blinded by tears, Manya groped for her child. Clasping him and sobbing, she ran for her last refuge—the Bernatovitch home. When she finally reached it, the door was bolted. She banged the knocker sharply and kicked at the door. Valodya was now unconscious and blue. When she got no reply, she became delirious. She let the baby slip to the porch floor and continued kicking and screaming until a vocal cord ruptured. Then, mutely, she collapsed.

*I*srael's experience, meanwhile, was no less a nightmare than Manya's. Believing that he and Manya had only been temporarily separated, he had run straight to the Bernatovitches'—clear across town. He was certain that Manya would go there since it was the prearranged plan.

As Israel ran, he constantly had to hide in doorways and behind buildings. Attackers were everywhere in the streets. As he dodged, hid, and ran, he had repeated to himself, over and over, "Of course she went to Madame Bernatovitch because of the bundle—where else could she hide?"

His crippled feet became wings, but his speed was for nothing. When he reached the Bernatovitch house, he found it darkened. He called and called, but there was no response. He was crying now, broken and alone. He had no reserve strength on which to draw. After having won so much, he could not accept that all was now lost.

In the chaos that swept the town, the chances were one in a million that he would find Manya and his son alive. He had no faith that he could be that lucky. Only Manya and Valodya could rescue him from his despair. Where in this burning purgatory could they have gone?

Suddenly, he had another idea. Perhaps Manya had gone

to Marina's house! It wasn't too far from where they must have separated. Surely, this was the closest place of shelter. With soaring hope, he turned abruptly and ran off.

A blessing—the house was lighted! He knocked at the door and as it opened, he heard drunken laughter. Marina only opened the door a crack. When she saw Israel, color swept her face. She asked in a brash voice, "What the hell are you doing here? Jews are dying all over the place. You'd better get away from here or you may join the dead. But wait on the bench. I'll bring you some vodka first."

As she turned into the house, he spotted his own samovar and candlesticks on her table. In stunned disbelief he took the vodka and left. Evidently, she thought that this night would see the last of him, and that she might as well have his belongings, instead of the bandits.

Well then, he thought—maybe the synagogue. Manya might have gone there. His tired feet began to pick up speed. This was positively his last hope. He ran over bodies and through dense clouds of smoke. As he approached the synagogue with a pounding heart, he saw horses in the sanctuary, and here and there he spotted a Ukrainian soldier. The men were loud and filled with drink. There was no refuge here—not for his wife or child, and not for him. His search was brought to an abrupt end. Now was the time to surrender. He was robbed of all will.

Silently he spoke to God. "I don't know why you are so displeased with me, but your anger is awesome. I must be a greater sinner than I realize. But what sins have Manya and Valodya committed? Why should they suffer? Why don't you take my life? I have no fear of death—I welcome it now. Living will cause me far greater suffering. I have no wish to exist without my family."

Israel cried without restraint, until his eyes and nose were swollen and red. He had taken leave of his senses, and he walked the streets uncaring, unseeing. But he was not alone. As he walked aimlessly, he bumped into others who were hysterical and in shock, babbling incoherently.

At last, a hand reached out and stopped him. "Israel, Israel, get a hold of yourself."

It was Kushner, the dry goods merchant who had alerted the Abramsons earlier that evening. He and his friends had found a good hiding place, and they were leaving for Romania in a few days—if they lived that long. Already, some of the group had perished. He calmed Israel and took him to his secret retreat. There Israel retold his nightmare from beginning to end. Tomorrow, he told Kushner's friends, he would make the rounds looking for Manya and Valodya, dead or alive.

A voice in the group murmured sadly, "You don't have to search, Israel. I have seen them." The man's tone was revealing, and his face held no joy. "Manya and Valodya were lying dead on the frozen lake," he continued. "People were trying to identify their loved ones, and the whole area was aglow with torches. Although I was several feet away from them, I recognized your wife and baby. I am sure it was they."

Israel jumped up, ready to run and see for himself, but he was forcibly restrained. The group convinced him that going to the lake would be fruitless.

"Don't go," a neighbor begged. "The dogs were already sniffing the bodies, and the funeral carts were there. By now all the bodies must have been taken away."

Now, Israel's grief was so profound that he had a shaking fit. For hours, he cried for his loved ones.

Finally Kushner said, "My good brother, make peace with the past and come away with us. The passage is already paid, and you can take the place of one of the dead."

Reluctantly, Israel agreed. There was a *minyan* of men present, and they recited *Kaddish* for the dead. After that, he felt resigned and ready to depart.

When things had quieted down outside, Israel ventured to the home of the Bernatovitches. He wanted, at least, to claim his family's last few possessions. To avoid being recognized as a Jew on the streets, he wore a *swita,* or crude peasant robe, and a hat. As he knocked on the imposing door of the Bernatovitch home, he heard a scramble inside. He waited, but there was no response to his knocks and calls. Again he banged, knowing that someone was inside. But still there was no reply.

"What is this?" he exclaimed. Could Bernatovitch have hardened his heart against Israel? And even if he had, how could he recognize Israel in his disguise? Israel could not believe that his friends would ignore him. He continued to thump on the door with his boot and with the staff in his hand, and began shouting.

Inside, a terrified woman, alone in the grand house, thought her heart would burst. She pushed the curtain aside just a bit to peek at the crudely dressed peasant outside. She had been ordered not to let anyone in, as it could mean her death and a death sentence for all those responsible for her being there.

But the voice—the voice was familiar. It was so like the voice for which her soul cried out. She felt that her flesh would separate from her bones, so torn was she between the fear of making a mistake and her desire to believe that the insistent stranger was her own love.

In a reckless moment, she succumbed and opened the door. At the sight of her, Israel shrieked and fainted. As his hat fell away, Manya instantly recognized her husband.

After Manya had helped Israel inside and had revived him with brandy, they clung to each other in amazement. He was so confused and dazed that she had to tell him the details of her torment and rescue over and over. Obviously the man who thought he had seen Manya and Valodya on the lake was very much mistaken. She described everything: seeking refuge in the synagogue, Valodya's fall, the saber blow from the soldier, and fainting before the Bernatovitches could answer the door. Then she told Israel how the Bernatovitches had paid a doctor in gold rubles to stitch Valodya's head and how they had bribed the servants to keep them quiet. She spoke of her friends with reverence for their honor and devotion. She omitted no incident, except, of course, her own desertion of that destitute orphan on the night of the pogrom.

Israel, for his part, told Manya everything he had been through. When he told her about Marina, her mouth fell open in astonishment. Then her shock turned to anger.

"My God, Israel," she cried, "What do they want of us? Why is all Russia incited against us?"

For the second time in their lives together, they had experienced a miracle of reunion that was almost beyond belief. At first they could only embrace mutely, overwhelmed with the joy of having found one another. Slowly, however, they both regained their balance and began to see the realities of their situation. They were trapped in Manistritch. Valodya was recovering, but he was in no condition to be moved. Fortunately, the Bernatovitches rejoiced to find Israel alive and unharmed. They insisted that the Abramsons remain with them, at least until Valodya was able to travel. They gave Israel a loaded gun and told him to take it with him whenever he left the house.

Israel cautiously began to venture about town with his peasant costume and gun for protection. He felt compelled to visit the street where his drugstore had been, though his business and home were now totally demolished. As he stood facing the burned debris, his whole being shrivelled.

A passerby hesitantly asked, "Israel Abramson?"

Israel turned to see a man who was also a pharmacist. They fell into each other's arms and wept. Although this man had been Israel's strongest competitor, now he was simply a fellow Jew, commiserating. His own property had not been touched, and his entire family was unscathed. But he agonized for the suffering of his neighbor. He implored Israel to bring Manya and Valodya and to stay with him. Israel accepted the kind offer, because it would give him a chance to work and to collect enough money for the trip to Talne. He and Manya had already decided that they would have to return there as soon as possible. But they needed money, and it was now impossible to retrieve their buried gold from beneath the burned rubble of their home.

When they were able to move Valodya, Manya, Israel, and the baby joined the pharmacist's family. The Abramsons lived with the family for several weeks until, against the wishes of their hosts, they left for Talne. Their departure was fortunate, for within hours after the Abramsons left Manistritch, early in April 1920, the pharmacist and his entire family were murdered in their beds by Petlura's men.

But the Abramsons also faced danger on the road, for roving bands of Ukrainian nationalists were terrorizing travelers. Although no one was absolutely safe on the highway, Jews were especially vulnerable. Both Manya and Israel wore dirty peasant *switas* to conceal their identities. The couple took trains and carts or walked, whichever was most expedient. When they rode the train, it would stop at each station, and Israel and other passengers would go into the woods to fetch wood for fuel. The process took forever. By the time they reached Talne, Manya was starved and exhausted. Poor Valodya was pale and wan, a robust infant no more. At the Talne train station, Israel suggested that Manya sit in a corner of the waiting area while he went to see if any of the Polevois were still alive. If possible. he would bring a wagon back for her and the baby. For protection, he tucked the gun in her hand.

Miraculously, the Polevois were alive and well. When they saw Israel, they wept for joy and shouted prayers of thanksgiving. But they would not let him return for Manya. They insisted that he eat and rest while Boorah engaged a wagon driver and went to meet his sister and nephew.

At the station, Manya watched the wagon pull into sight and saw Boorah anxiously scan the waiting area. But he did not even recognize her! When he started to leave, Manya screamed, "Boorah, Boorah, it's me, Manya!"

As Boorah beheld the disheveled creature he had bypassed, he moaned, "Manya, sweet girl! This can't be you. I can't believe you've come to this."

They fell into each other's arms, sobbing with mixed sadness and relief. Weakly, Manya got into the wagon with Valodya in her arms. Then, as they rode through the streets, the wagon driver shouted to all within earshot. "Yosel Polevoi's daughter and her child are alive!" Soon a joyful procession followed them home.

$\mathcal{M}$anya, Israel, and Valodya remained in Yosel's home for over a month, recovering their strength. When they were well and strong again, Israel decided that he and Manya should go to Odessa. He desperately wanted to find out what had become of his mother and his brother Samuel. Samuel's wife, Fania, had relatives in Odessa who would know.

Then, too, Israel thought that Grisha Skliar, Fania's uncle, might help him to find work in Odessa. In Talne there was no employment, and he could not allow the Polevois to continue supporting his family. Despite the Polevois' opposition, the couple decided to strike out on their own. They both reassured the Polevois that if this did not work out well, they would return. But Israel had privately declared to Manya that unless matters developed favorably in Odessa, he was ready to consider emigrating to America. After what Manya had gone through, she didn't care where they went, as long as they could live in peace. Besides, she secretly believed that her parents would eventually emigrate, too. Then, she thought, they would all be together again.

In Odessa, many pharmacists remembered Israel's skill, and he soon found a job and located a tiny flat nearby. He learned from Grisha that his mother and Samuel's family had survived a terrible pogrom in Varpnovica, their hometown.

Apparently, the Jewish men of the village had been rounded up to be shot, and Samuel had been among those caught. When the shots had been fired, however, he had not been wounded. But he had let himself fall with the others, and had lain there until dark, long after the final moans of those suffering were silenced. When he had returned to his home in the middle of the night, he had learned that Petlura's soldiers had barged into his house and cornered Fania and the three children—Adela, William, and the infant Yasha. The soldiers had ransacked the house but, spent from earlier atrocities, they had heeded Adela's pleas not to hurt them.

Israel's mother, meanwhile, had unsuspectingly entered the home of relatives, only to find that they had all been executed. Afraid to leave the house and risk her life in the streets, she had covered her body with their warm blood and had lain among the victims for hours. She had reasoned that if bandits reentered, they would be gone in a hurry at the sight of the bloody massacre.

After comparing notes and realizing how close they all had come to being killed, Samuel's family had decided to leave Russia. But Grisha did not know the particulars of their final arrangements. So Israel and Manya agreed to go to Varpnovica to learn the specifics.

Now another problem arose. They could not leave immediately, for Valodya was not faring well at all. The child's wounds were not healing, and Manya and Israel were getting very worried about his condition. He had a low fever and was very cranky—a sure sign of illness in Valodya. Manya was very concerned about hygiene and had tried to keep his head wound sterile. But Valodya had two festered boils on his scalp and needed surgery. So the Abramsons decided to take him to Yavongolititz Hospital, a German hospital about 10 miles away. Taking turns carrying the sick child, Manya and Israel trudged the distance, trying to comfort the whining bundle. At Yavongolititz, the doctors told the frightened parents that treating Valodya would be a simple procedure, but that no anesthesia was available. The surgery would have to be performed without it!

"No, no!" screamed Manya, and she ran from the examining room.

To Israel, the doctor said compassionately, "If you change your mind, bring him back tomorrow. He doesn't have a good chance even with the surgery, but without it, he has none at all."

Reluctantly, after a tearful debate, Manya agreed that Valodya must have the operation. When they arrived at the hospital the next day, she was in anguish. Israel had given her some strong vodka to calm her, but even so, she could not get a grip on her nerves. While in the hospital waiting room, she wrung her hands and shook her head continuously, unable to cry or even pray. In a stupor, she waited.

Israel stayed with Valodya during the operation. It was crudely done, at best. The child had not even been prepared in a special gown, and his own clothes became bloodsoaked. When at last they left the hospital, Valodya was limp and purple in Israel's arms. But soon afterwards, the child began to respond. Within a few months after the terrible ordeal, the healing was complete.

When the Abramsons were certain that Valodya was out of danger, they made arrangements for the trip to Varpnovica. Full of hope, they gathered their few bundles and embarked on their journey. Once in Varpnovica, they learned that all of the Abramsons had gone to Soroki, a town in Bessarabia, Romania. They planned to stay at the home of Fania's parents, the Skliars, who were wealthy and living in comfort and peace. Israel and Manya decided to go there too, and from there to make plans for emigrating to America. They had finally agreed that they could make no life in Russia with conditions as they were.

Israel made plans for them to be smuggled across the Dniester River from Tzakinyifka, in Russian Ukraine, to a point near the town of Soroki. Their dangerous passage would be made quickly and quietly, under cover of night.

At the appointed time, Israel and Manya took Valodya to the riverfront and stood there together on Russian soil for the last time, awaiting a signal from the other side that would tell them the Romanian river guards were not about. After the signal came, a small boat glided quietly out of the shadows. The trio made ready to get in, but to their dismay the boat captain began to argue with Israel. The couple were wearing new clothes (the only ones they owned), and the smugglers who operated the boat now insisted on more money than had previously been agreed upon. They flatly refused to get the Abramsons across unless their new demands were met. Israel, however, could not pay the additional sum required. Finally, the smugglers agreed to hold Manya and Valodya hostage in a storage shack and to take Israel across alone. Israel would then locate the Skliars and return with the extra money, which would buy Manya's and Valodya's passage.

Soroki was about 25 miles from the point where Israel crossed the river. and the smugglers rode with him on horseback to the town to secure the cash. Only when their heavy demands were satisfied did they signal for Manya and Valodya to board the next night with a boatload of emigrants.

When the smugglers unlocked the shed door, they were greeted by a putrid odor. While Manya had dozed, Valodya had crept into an open sack of crab apples and had eaten so many that he had become ill. He had suffered spasms of violent cramps and diarrhea all night, and confined as they were, Manya had not been able to properly clean and change the child. Tired and foul-smelling, mother and child boarded the boat with about a dozen other fleeing souls.

It was late November, and the night air was frigid. Icy sheets of rain smacked their faces as they waited for the open boat to get under way. Even with the extra payment, the captain was most unhappy about taking Manya and the child. He said it would he dangerous for the boy to utter a sound, for if a patrol heard it, it could mean the end of all of their lives. The captain insisted that Manya had to promise to throw Valodya in the river, should he begin to cry. Manya nodded in agreement, without, of course, meaning it at all. Valodya, still cramped but exhausted, slept.

The boat was in the middle of the river when Manya spotted Romania. In some village there, lights were shining all over town. She thought it must be a festival of some sort. As they went a little further, she could hear gypsy music in the distance. Turning back to the Russian shore, she saw quite another sight. A small *shtetl* was ablaze. Petlura's men had no doubt visited the village. Their signatures were glowing against the blackened sky.

"Good riddance." she whispered, shaking a fist at the shore —at the homeland that regarded her as a despised intruder. Then she raised her hand to her lips and gently blew a kiss to all that was familiar and loved.

"Good-bye, *shtetl,* forever."

Her small voice caused Valodya to stir. He started to wail. She had tried to protect him from the stinging rain as well as she could, but now he was thoroughly wet and cold, and he was letting her know about it.

His next bellow was drowned out by the captain's command, "Throw him in now." Narrowing his eyes, he added, "Or I'll throw you both in."

Manya tore at her clothes and pressed Valodya to her breast. Immediately the child began to suckle, and silence was restored. Manya's nerves were taut until the boat reached the shore and she saw Israel waiting with his mother, Samuel, and Fania. The group embraced in a confusion of joy and salty tears.

Her last ordeal had left Manya completely demoralized and spent. She propped herself against the feather quilt bundles in the Skliars' carriage and wept and slept throughout the ride back to Soroki.

But the healing effects of time slowly began to work in Manya's favor. After spending a few weeks with the Skliars, she and Israel took heart and dared to dream of a brighter future in America—"the golden land." It was a time of planning, preparing, and waiting. Herman, Israel's brother from Philadelphia, wrote that he and their brother Benjamin were trying to make arrangements through HIAS (the Hebrew Immigrant Aid Society) for their entry into the United States, but that the Abramsons would first have to get to Liverpool, England. Other emigrants in Soroki were going to Antwerp, Belgium, and the Abramsons thought it might be easier to get to England from there. So they decided to end their sojourn in Soroki and to join the band of refugees bound for Belgium.

When it came time for Manya and Israel to say their last farewells to their relatives, Samuel tenderly embraced Manya. He kissed her trembling lips and said, "May God be with you and give you the chance to live a life that will bring honor to your ancestors. May your zeyda in heaven, Shmuel Ber, continue to pray for you."

Israel and Manya's eyes met, and they acknowledged his prayer with a silent pledge. They had indeed been blessed with a second chance for life, and the gift of their survival had brought with it a great responsibility. With God's help and with Torah for guidance and inspiration, their lives would become a beacon to light the way for Valodya and the children they hoped yet to have.

I will be glad and rejoice

    in Thy loving kindness;

  For Thou hast seen

    mine affliction,

  Thou hast taken cognizance of

    the troubles of my soul,

And Thou has not given me over

    into the hand of the enemy;

  Thou has set my feet in a broad

    place.

                      Psalms 31: 7-8

EPILOGUE

Like so many Jews left homeless and destitute after the Russian Revolution, Manya, Israel, and Valodya found a haven in the United States with the aid of the Hebrew Immigrant Aid Society, an organization formed during World War I. They landed at Ellis Island in 1921. Manya's uncle, Israel Polevoi, settled them in Mt. Pleasant, Pennsylvania, a small mining town near his home, and helped them open a dry goods store. They were the only Jewish immigrants in the town.

In 1929 Manya and Israel moved to South Philadelphia with their sons, William (Valodya), Robert, and Seymour. Here, for the first time in America, they were among other Jewish immigrants and were no longer isolated. People in this community spoke Yiddish in the shops, sold kosher food, and practiced traditional Judaism in the synagogues. I was born in Philadelphia and named Bettyanne (Brucha Channa) after my valiant great-grandmother and my young aunt.

Most of the family left behind in Ukraine perished. After the Revolution, Bubba Brucha decided that she had seen enough for a lifetime and retired to her bed to die. Channa Polevoi died in her early twenties after escaping from drunken Russian youths who attempted to rape her. Most probably she suffered a fatal asthma attack. My uncle Mikhail was killed in World War II while serving in the Russian Army. His wife, daughter, and her family eventually emigrated to Israel. Pavlusha was killed in the Holocaust. Ruchel, an ardent Communist until she died, lived in Russia with her daughter. My uncle Boorah, now elderly and frail, is still in Russia.

In 1946 my mother received a tragic letter from Uncle Boorah. He informed her that her beloved parents, Leah and Yosel, had been victims of the Holocaust. Her venerated father was hung by his thumbs in the village square until he died, a special torture inflicted on him as a Jewish community leader. Her beautiful, gentle mother was shot to death, ignobly, beside a cattle car. My mother kept Boorah's letter until her death.

After struggling financially for years, my parents achieved a comfortable middle-class life. Congregation Beth Am Israel became the core of their social and religious activities. My father served on the Congregation's Ritual Committee and was president of the Tolner-Dubner Brotherhood Association. Sadly, he died on December 6, 1957, shortly after my 23rd birthday. We remember my father as a gregarious, accepting, warmhearted human being who gave his family unconditional love. He is sorely missed.

My mother worked 20 years as a sewing machine operator in the garment industry as well as involving herself closely with her children and grandchildren. She devoted the rest of her energies to Zionist volunteer work. She was a member of Hadassah and Pioneer Women (now called Na'Amat), and served as secretary to the Philadelphia Auxiliary of the General Israel Orphans Home in Jerusalem.

Through Pioneer Women, my mother met the renowned Israeli author and community activist, Rivka Guber. Mrs. Guber introduced my mother to Kfar Achim, a village in the Negev Desert inhabited solely by Holocaust survivors.

In 1963 my mother financed the renovation of the village's bombed-out cultural center. The cultural center was then dedicated to the memory of her martyred parents. My mother also raised funds for a park surrounding the center. In appreciation, the villagers named the park Gan Miryam, or "Garden of Miriam," in her honor.

My mother's ties to the General Israel Orphans Home, Kfar Achim, and her beloved friend Rivka Guber added a vitality to her later years. These activities fulfilled the youthful idealism nurtured many years earlier in Talne.

My openhearted mother taught me the importance of setting wise priorities, the value of community involvement, and the special joy of laughter. As a devoted and loving wife, mother, and grandmother whose spirit ennobled all who knew her, Manya faced uncommon trials with uncommon grace. She was truly a woman of valor.

Leaving the aching hearts of her family behind, Manya died on June 17, 1975. May her memory be blessed.

The last picture of Leah and Yosel Polevoi taken before they were killed by the Nazis during World War II

Opposite above: *Manya and Israel had relatives who had preceded them to the United States. Manya's uncle Israel Polevoi left Russia when he was a young man.*

Opposite below: *Manya's aunt Raisel and her husband, Frank Olschanetzki (Olson), also settled in the United States in the early 20th century.*

Above left: *Benjamin Abramson, Israel's brother, was a medical student at Ohio State University in 1910.*

Above right: *Manya's uncle Zeylik, Yosel's oldest brother, fled to the United States in 1911.*

Left: *This picture of Manya, Israel, and Valodya was taken shortly after their arrival in the United States in 1921.*

Right: *William (Valodya) Abramson on his first day of school in 1924*

102

Left: *Manya, Israel, and their three sons in 1930:* (from left to right) *Robert, Seymour, and William*

Right: *Manya and her daughter, Bettyanne, 1935*

Above: *Members of the Polevoi family who remained in Russia:* (standing left to right) *Mikhail and Ruchel's daughter, Meilya;* (seated left to right) *Boorah and Channa. This picture was taken in 1925.*

Below: *Meilya* (left) *and her cousin Leonid, Boorah's son*

Above: *Mikhail and his wife, Fania, with their son, Israel. Mikhail was killed in battle during World War II.*

Below left: *Boorah Polevoi and his wife, Fania, live in Russia today.*

Below right: *Boorah's son, Leonid, and his wife, Meilya, are also Russian citizens. Both are eye doctors.*

As a direct result of the 1978 publication of *Manya's Story,*
I was contacted by many Polevoi relations who had discovered family photographs in the book. I have now located over
200 cousins, including 35 recent Russian emigrants. The
reconnection of this extended family of Russian-American
Jews has shown how important the remembrance of our
shared history is to all of us.

Known descendants of
  Yosel and Leah Polevoi:

Abramson, Chad
Abramson, Keevan
Abramson, Lisa
Abramson, Marlene Koenig
Abramson, Stephen
Abramson, William
Avanessov, Emily
Avanessov, Marina Polevoy
Avanessov, Dr. Valentin
Devita, Angelo
Devita, Charles Jacob
Devita, Elizabeth Manya
  Rachel
Devita, Heidi Gray
Gateman, Alexander
Gateman, Edward
Gateman, Ella
Gateman, Igor
Gellman, Alexander
Gellman, Danielle
Gellman, Polina
Gray, Aaron Michael
Gray, Bettyanne
Gray, Donald
Gray, Donna Tolmie
Gray, Ellis
Gray, Jacob Matthew
Gray, Mason Alexander
Lipschutz, Jacklyn Mandy
Lipschutz, Tara Dawn
Nelson, Daniel
Nelson, Kathy
Nelson, Maxine
Nelson, Seymour
Nelson, Shawn

Pekar, Alexander
Pekar, Anna Polevoy
Pekar, David
Pekar, Michael
Pekar, Stanislav
Pekar, Tanya
Polevoy, Demitry
Polevoy, Fania
Polevoy, Israel
Polevoy, Lena
Waskow, Dan
Waskow, Debi

Known descendants of
  Raisel (Polevoi) and
  Frank Olson:

Crutch, Fredric
Crutch, Mechelle
Crutch, Rina
Manheim, Allison Renee
Manheim, Carolyn Beth
  Olson
Manheim, Jonathan
  Geoffrey
Manheim, Michael Philip
Muravchik, Arlene Olson
Muravchik, Rose
Muravchik, Dr. Stanley
Miller, A. T.
Olson, Albert L.
Olson, Alexis
Olson, Audrey Becker
Olson, Benjamin Andrew
Olson, Edward Aaron
Olson, Emily Rose

Olson, Frances
Olson, Francine Laurel
Olson, Franklin Jay
Olson, Irene
Olson, Irving J.
Olson, Mark Luck
Olson, Miriam Klein
Olson, Norman J.
Olson, Philip
Olson, Remy
Olson, Renee
Olson, Ruth Sydel Bogen
Olson, Sidney
Olson, Stuart
Olson, Sylvia
Schoenberger, William
Stolow, Linda

Known descendants of
  Yankel and Pearl Polevoi:

Polevoy, Alexander
Polevoy, Alexander Lazar
Polevoy, Ann
Polevoy, Demitri
Polevoy, Igor
Polevoy, Irina
Polevoy, Kirill
Polevoy, Lazar
Polevoy, Margaret
Polevoy, Michael
Polevoy, Polina
Polevoy, Savily
Polevoy, Valentina
Polevoy, Vladimir
Polevoy, Vladislav

GLOSSARY
of Yiddish and Hebrew Terms

bar mitzvah — A ceremony celebrating a boy's becoming a full member of the Jewish community at the age of 13

ben zokher — A celebration held on the first Sabbath eve after the birth of a son

bris — The act and ceremony of circumcision, symbolizing a male infant's reception into the Jewish community. In Hebrew, "brith" means covenant. Also termed **brit milah** ("covenant by circumcision").

bubba — Grandmother

challah — A twisted loaf of bread served on the Sabbath and on holidays

chuppah — A ceremonial canopy used in a wedding ceremony

gabai — A synagogue president or leader (plural, **gaboyim**)

goyim — Gentiles

hamantashen — A traditional three-cornered Purim pastry

Hamotzee — A blessing said over bread

Kaddish — A memorial prayer for the dead

Kiddush — A blessing said over a cup of wine, consecrating the Sabbath or a holiday

minyan — A quorum of 10 males needed for public religious services

Mishnah — A part of the Talmud dealing with collections of oral laws

mishpucha	Family
mitzvah	A divine commandment or a good deed (plural, **mitzvoth**)
mohel	The person who performs a circumcision
Purim	A holiday commemorating the defeat of the tyrannical Haman, described in the Book of Esther
sachud	Reign of terror
sandek	The person who holds an infant during the circumcision ceremony
seudah	A festival meal, such as a wedding seudah or Purim seudah
Shabbos	The Jewish Sabbath, lasting from sunset on Friday until sunset on Saturday
shtetl	A small village; a typical Jewish community in eastern Europe
shtuut balabos	Town leader or city boss
swita	A crude peasant robe
Talmud	A written collection of oral laws, teachings, customs, and interpretations of laws cited in the Torah
Torah	The five books of Moses; the first five books of the Christian Bible. The word also refers to scrolls on which the Torah is inscribed.
Vey-iz-meer	"Woe is me."
zeyda	Grandfather

Bettyanne Gray is the recipient of the Lewis Carroll Shelf Award for the original edition of *Manya's Story*. She holds a bachelor's degree in Jewish studies from Gratz College where she has taught literature and history in the high school department since 1981. Ms. Gray has also lectured and taught adult courses in Holocaust and Jewish studies throughout the Philadelphia area. Her stories and articles have appeared in *Forward, Jewish Exponent, Jewish Spectator,* and *Midstream*. She and her husband, Donald Gray, have three children, Ellis, Heidi, and Debi, and are the proud grandparents of Charles, Aaron, Jacob, Elizabeth Rachel, and Mason Alexander.